D1324421

THE
KENNEDYS
&
VIETNAM

THE
KENNEDYS
&
VIETNAM

Edited by John Galloway

Adjunct Assistant Professor of Political Science,
Hunter College of the City of New York

FACTS ON FILE, INC.　　　　　　　NEW YORK

THE
KENNEDYS
&
VIETNAM

Also by John Galloway: The Gulf of Tonkin Resolution

CONTENTS

i

ROBERT FRANCIS KENNEDY

EDWARD MOORE KENNEDY

INTRODUCTION

M UCH HAS BEEN WRITTEN about the brothers John F. Kennedy, Robert F. Kennedy and Edward M. Kennedy. John Kennedy was President when the U.S. was first becoming seriously involved in Vietnam, and he was assassinated at a time when this involvement was growing. Robert Kennedy had been a member of the cabinet of his brother and his brother's successor, and his advice was known to have been influential in the formation of U.S. policy on Vietnam. By the time he too was assassinated, however, Robert Kennedy had broken with the Administration on the Vietnam issue and was a Presidential candidate vehemently opposed to U.S. activities in Vietnam. Edward Kennedy appeared to many observers to be a logical successor to Robert both as a potential President and as a leader in the opposition to the Administration's Vietnam policy.

A great deal of the material written about the Kennedys, therefore, has dealt with their relationship to the war in Vietnam. Most of the information published about the Kennedys and Vietnam, however, comes from people closely identified with one or more of the Kennedys or from persons seemingly intent on destroying the Kennedy reputation. In neither case can the reader expect the degree of objectivity and fairness that characterizes true scholarship. An information gap has, therefore, been created on the subject of the Kennedys and Vietnam.

This book attempts to fill that void, at least in part, pending the publication of fuller and more definitive accounts. This volume seeks neither to praise nor to damn the Kennedys. It doesn't try to prove anything. In presenting this fairly detailed account of the Kennedys and Vietnam, an attempt was made only to bring together the information currently available and thereby to assist the reader in forming his own conclusions. Thanks are due—and herewith extended—to the staffs of the National Archives & Records Service and of the John F. Kennedy Library in Waltham, Mass. and Washington, D.C. for their assistance.

JOHN
FITZGERALD
KENNEDY

John Fitzgerald Kennedy

John F. Kennedy represented the 11th Massachusetts Congressional District in the U.S. House of Representatives from 1947 to 1952. From 1953 to 1960 he was a U.S. Senator from Massachusetts. During his 12 years in the House and Senate John Kennedy displayed more interest in Indochina and Vietnam than most of his House and Senate colleagues.

Kennedy was 29 years old when he was first elected to the House of Representatives. During his initial 2 years in Congress he seldom spoke on foreign affairs. His first major foreign policy pronouncements were delivered in Jan. 1950. His subject was the Communist overthrow of the Nationalist government of Chiang Kai-shek in China.

Kennedy received permission to address the House of Representatives for one minute Jan. 25, 1950. This is what he said: "Mr. Speaker, over this weekend we have learned the extent of the disaster that has befallen China and the United States. The responsibility for the failure of our foreign policy in the Far East rests squarely with the White House and the Department of State. The continued insistence that aid would not be forthcoming, unless a coalition government with the Communists were formed, was a crippling blow to the National Government. So concerned were our diplomats and their advisers, the [Owen] Lattimores and the [John] Fairbanks, with the imperfection of the democratic system in China after 20 years of war and the tales of corruption in high places that they lost sight of our tremendous stake in a non-Communist China.... This House must now assume the responsibility of preventing the onrushing tide of communism from engulfing all of Asia."

In a speech delivered 5 days later, in Salem, Mass. Jan. 30, Kennedy repeated these charges and elaborated on them: "At the Yalta Conference in 1945 a sick Roosevelt, with the advice of Gen. [George C.] Marshall and other chiefs of staff, gave the Kurile Islands as well as the control of various strategic Chinese ports, such as Port Arthur and Dairen, to the Soviet Union.... When the armies of Soviet Russia withdrew from Manchuria they left Chinese Communists in control of this area and in possession of great masses of Japanese war material.... There were those who claimed, and still claim, that Chinese communism was not really communism at all but merely an advanced agrarian movement which did not take directions from Moscow.... This is the tragic story of China, whose freedom we once fought to preserve. What our young men had saved, our diplomats and our President have frittered away."

JFK Visits Indochina, Predicts French Defeat

John Kennedy, accompanied by his brother Robert, travelled around the world in the fall of 1951. The trip took 7 weeks, 10 days of which were spent in Indochina. The U.S. government at that time considered the French effort against the Communist-led Viet Minh in Indochina to be part of the same struggle against international communism that the U.S. was waging against Communist North Korea following the invasion of South Korea in June 1950. In Vietnam John Kennedy asked the French commander in Indochina, Gen. Jean de Lattre de Tassigny, why the Vietnamese should be expected to fight the Viet Minh to keep their country part of France. Following his meeting with Kennedy, de Lattre sent a formal letter of complaint about the young Congressman to the American minister.

Reporting on his trip, Kennedy, in a radio broadcast Nov. 14, predicted disaster for the French in Indochina and suggested that the U.S. rely on Asian nationalism, rather than the French army, to halt communism in Southeast Asia.

"In Indochina," he said, "we have allied ourselves to the desperate effort of a French regime to hang on to the remnants of empire. There is no broad, general support of the native Vietnam government among the people of that area, and there will be none until the French give clear indications that, despite their gallantry, they are fighting not merely for themselves but for the sake of strengthening a non-Communist native government so that it can move safely toward independence. These Indochinese states are puppet states, French principalities with great resources but as typical examples of empire and of colonialism as can be found anywhere. To check the southern drive of communism makes sense but not only through reliance on the force of arms. The task is rather to build strong native non-Communist sentiment within these areas and rely on that as a spearhead of defense rather than upon the legions of Gen. de Lattre, brilliant though he may be. And to do this apart from and in defiance of innately nationalistic aims spells foredoomed failure. To the rising drive of nationalism, we have unfortunately become a friend of its enemy and as such its enemy and not its friend."

JFK Urges Independence for Indochinese

Appearing on NBC's "Meet the Press" Dec. 3, 1951, Kennedy urged the Truman Administration to pressure the French into agreeing to grant independence to the Indochinese.

"We [have] tied ourselves completely with the French," Kennedy said. "You can never defeat the Communist movement in Indochina until you get the support of the natives, and you won't get the support of the natives as long as they feel that the French are fighting the Communists in order to hold their own power there. And I think we shouldn't give the military assistance until the French clearly make an agreement with the natives that at the end of a certain time, when the Communists are defeated, that the French will pull out and give this country the right of self-determination and the right to govern themselves. Otherwise, this guerrilla war is just going to spread and grow, and we're going to finally get driven out of Southeast Asia."

Throughout the 1950s Kennedy was a leading critic of French imperialism in Indochina and Algeria. In the *New Republic* Oct. 13, 1952, a Harvard teaching fellow gave this summary of Kennedy's record on foreign affairs during his 6 years in the House: "The best which can be said is that he [Kennedy] almost always votes for Administration programs, though on one or 2 occasions he has been one of the few Northern Democrats to favor cuts in foreign aid. He talks more isolationist than he votes; again, he has admitted that this is related to his constituents, poor men with a deep suspicion that 'someone' on the top levels of government is betraying them and sending them off to die." The article concluded: "One can only hope that the educational experience of service in the U.S. Senate—plus probably ambitions for even higher office—will lead John F. Kennedy, like others before him, along the road to more enlightened public service."

During the Korean war Kennedy told a class at Harvard that he could see no reason for the U.S. to be fighting in Korea.

John Kennedy was elected to the Senate in 1952. In the course of a successful campaign against the incumbent Henry Cabot Lodge, Kennedy sought the conservative vote by attacking Lodge's record on foreign affairs. A 40-page campaign paper prepared by Kennedy's administrative assistant, Timothy J. (Ted) Reardon, stressed that "Kennedy has been an outspoken critic of many elements of the [Truman] Administration's foreign policy. In this respect, he has been much closer to the position of Taft than has Lodge. Indeed the latter has been at the head of the so-called bipartisan foreign policy parade since 1947." The paper concluded: "The outstanding question, of course, in his [Lodge's] case as well as the Administration's is why there has not been more of an awareness for strong anti-Communist policy in the Far East."

One of Kennedy's first major actions in the Senate was to offer an amendment to the mutual security (foreign aid) bill providing that U.S. aid funds for Indochina, "to the extent that it is feasible..., be administered in such a way [as] to encourage through all available means the freedom and independence desired by the peoples of the Associated States [of Indochina], including the intensification of the military training of the Vietnamese." The measure was defeated by a 67-13 vote.

Kennedy Backs 'Domino Theory'

Kennedy's foreign-aid amendment led to his first public espousal of the so-called "domino theory"—the thesis that the fall of one country to the Communists would trigger successive Communist victories in neighboring countries. According to this view, the surrounding countries would go down "like a row of dominoes."

Speaking on behalf of his amendment, Kennedy insisted in a June 30, 1953 Senate speech that the non-Communist Vietnamese could not be expected to fight the Viet Minh in order to save their country for the French. He called it essential that the Communists be defeated in Vietnam lest their success there lead to a Communist takeover of all of Southern Asia. Thereafter, until his death in 1963, Kennedy never publicly questioned the validity of the "domino theory."

In his June 30 speech, Kennedy said:

● "If France were to withdraw her troops today, Communists would overrun not only French Indochina but Southeast Asia. But it is because we want the war to be brought to a successful conclusion that we should insist on genuine independence. The war has been going on since 1946.... The position of the French is not improving."

● Regardless of what the U.S. and France were to do in Vietnam, "it is a truism that the war can never be successful unless large numbers of the people of Vietnam are won over from their sullen neutrality and open hostility to it and fully support its successful conclusion. This can never be done unless they are assured beyond doubt that complete independence will be theirs at the conclusion of the war."

● Many people argued that in 1945 Ho Chi Minh was "ripe for Titoism if the French had been willing to grant him sufficient political concessions. It is difficult to be convinced of this, although it is true that in Nov. 1945 he did dissolve the Indochinese Communist Party and took similar conciliatory steps to gain the support of a majority of the people. But his record as a leading and active world Communist figure argues against this theory of Titoism, and the seizure of control by the Communists in China at a later date would have placed him in a most difficult position if he had attempted to break his ties with Moscow...."

● "It is of basic importance, at a time when we authorize the expenditure of large sums of money so that the war may be brought to a successful conclusion, that we realize that conditions are present in the relationship between France and the Associated States [of Indochina] that make it difficult to win the wholehearted support of the natives in the struggle against the Communists. I strongly believe that the French cannot succeed in their mission in Indochina without giving concessions necessary to make the native army a reliable and crusading force...."

● "I do not believe that the French are fighting in Indochina wholly for material things.... Men like Gen. de Lattre fought for the honor of France; and the French now are fighting because they know if they retreat, all of Southeast Asia will go to the Communists—that their position in North Africa will become endangered and that the security of Metropolitan France itself will be threatened. Thus they fight on and deserve our wholehearted support."

● "But I believe it vital for the cause for which both of us fight that conditions be established there that will make it possible for the French to win—that will rally the support of native elements to take their share of the struggle.... If we do so, not only would the prospects of victory be substantially enhanced, but the position of the United States and France and of the whole Western alliance in Asia will be materially advanced in Asia."

Kennedy's next major statement on Vietnam was made in a speech delivered before the Cathederal Club in Brooklyn Jan. 21, 1954. In his speech, entitled "A Strong and Vigorous Foreign Policy," Kennedy criticized the foreign policy of Pres. Eisenhower and his Secretary of State, John Foster Dulles.

Again Kennedy emphasized the strategic importance of Vietnam: "All observers agree that it is vital to the security of all of Southeast Asia that Indochina remain free from Communist domination, for if Indochina should be lost, undoubtedly, within a short time, Burma, Thailand, Malaya and Indonesia and other now independent states might fall under the control of the Communist bloc in a series of chain reactions. Such an occurrence obviously would have the most serious consequences for all the Middle East and Europe, and indeed for our own security. Thus, French Indochina may well be the keystone to the defense of all of Asia."

Kennedy claimed, moreover, that Eisenhower and Dulles had failed to consider alternatives to their policy of massive retaliation: "We must ask how the new Dulles policy and its dependence upon the threat of atomic retaliation will fare in these areas of guerrilla warfare. At what point would the threat of atomic weapons be used in the struggles in Southeast Asia ...?"

Kennedy said in this Jan. 21 address:

"If the Chinese do not intervene directly [in Indochina], and merely increase their supplies to the native Communist forces, and send informal 'volunteer' missions to assist in the training of troops and the handling of more complicated equipment, at what point would it ever be possible for us, in the words of Secy. Dulles, to employ 'massive retaliatory power'? It seems to me that we could be placed in a most difficult position of either giving no aid at all of the kind that is necessary to bring victory to us in the area, or the wrong kind of aid which would alienate the people of great sections of the world who might feel the remedy was worse than the disease.

"Of course, Mr. Dulles feels that the threat of attack will prevent the brush fires from starting far more effectively than could our subsequent efforts to assist the forces of freedom in each of these areas against the well-entrenched Communist guerrilla or native armies. But once the brush fire begins to spread, and particularly if it spreads through a series of localized combustions, then the new policy might be confronted with a serious dilemma."

In passing, Kennedy noted that "Indochina is probably the only country in the world where many observers believe the Communist-led element would win a free election."

PRELUDE TO U.S. INTERVENTION: 1954-60

JFK Suggests Conditions for U.S. Intervention

The French war effort in Vietnam collapsed in the spring of 1954 after the Viet Minh overran the French stronghold at Dien Bien Phu following a successful 56-day siege. While Dien Bien Phu was on the verge of collapse, Kennedy told the Senate Apr. 6 that it would be futile for the U.S. and its allies to intervene militarily in Indochina unless France changed the current "contractual relationships" between France and Indochina.

Kennedy said: "Certainly, I, for one, favor a policy of 'united action' by many nations whenever necessary to achieve a military and political victory for the Free World in that area, realizing full well that it may eventually require some commitment of our manpower. But to pour money, material and men into the jungles of Indochina without at least a remote prospect of victory would be dangerously futile and self-destructive.... The hard truth of the matter is, first, that without the wholehearted support of the peoples of the Associated States, without a reliable and crusading native army with a dependable officer corps, a military victory, even with American support, in that area is difficult, if not impossible, of achievement; and 2d, that the support of the people of that area cannot be obtained without a change in the contractual relationships which presently exist between the Associated States and the French Union."

Kennedy Apr. 14 repeated his contention that only "an effective native army" was capable of defeating the Communists in Vietnam. Addressing the Senate, Kennedy said:

"It is far more likely that the war will continue to go as it has been going, without overt Chinese aggression; and the French will become more discouraged and will refuse to make the political concessions which would permit the raising of an effective native army. Therefore, it seems to me that the conversations which are now going on with respect to building a system of mutual agreements for action in Indochina do not approach the heart of the problem at all.... What is needed far more to fight Communist aggression in Indochina is an effective native army to meet other native armies. Guarantees to come to the aid of Indochina, if the Chinese Communist armies cross the northern frontier, are helpful but not the primary requirements as of now. I am concerned that, in Secy. Dulles' desire to build up a coalition among the Philippines, Thailand, New Zealand, and Australia, we may lose sight of the main problem, which is the raising of an effective native army in Indochina."

11

Vietnam's Division Supported

Unlike some other Senators, Kennedy indicated that he was prepared to accept the division of Vietnam as a price of ending the war between France and the Viet Minh. Speaking before the Executives Club in Chicago May 28, Kennedy suggested, however, that it would not be feasible for the U.S. to intervene militarily in Indochina should the Communists refuse such a solution at the talks then taking place in Geneva. Kennedy said:

● "We may hope that the Communists, who would be necessarily concerned about a major war in the Far East the end of which they cannot foresee, will come to terms in Indochina. Present deliberations center about the possibility of a cease-fire and partition along the 16th Parallel, with Communist recognition of the security of Laos and Cambodia. This might permit the allies to establish a defensive pact solidifying their determination to repel, by whatever means are necessary, any Communist advances beyond that line."

● U.S. miscalculations in Indochina included the failure "to recognize the nature and significance of the independence movement in Indochina" and the U.S.' undue reliance on nuclear retaliation. "On the one hand, the importance of Vietnamese spirit and the traditions of our own policy motivated our desire for a French grant of independence. On the other hand, a strong body of opinion within our Department of State argued that the French would withdraw from the struggle, with disastrous results, if the ties binding Indochina to the French Union were severed. Seeking a rationalization by which to escape from this dilemma while preventing a French withdrawal, the United States, under Democratic as well as Republican administrations, chose to support the myth—and it was no more than a myth—that the Associated States of Cambodia, Laos and Vietnam were genuinely independent."

● "Our reduction of strength for resistance in so-called brush-fire wars, while threatening atomic retaliation, has in effect invited expansion by the Communists in areas such as Indochina through those techniques which they deem not sufficiently offensive to induce us to risk the atomic warfare for which we are so ill prepared defensively.... For if the United States can meet aggression only by risking hydrogen warfare, we hand an advantage to the aggressor nation willing to achieve its conquest by methods short of those inducing us to take that risk. In short, we must reverse our air cuts and our new-look military cuts and place national security ahead of balancing the budget."

JFK Denies Opposing U.S. Intervention

Kennedy denied July 8, 1954 that any Senate Democrat had "absolutely opposed" a U.S. military intervention in Indochina during the April (Dien Bien Phu) crisis. Rather, Kennedy asserted, "what they said was that they would not support U.S. intervention in Indochina unless certain conditions were met. Those conditions were 3 in number. One was independence for Indochina. The 2d was a united effort and action by other Asiatic powers in Indochina. The 3d was that the French be willing to continue the struggle. The meeting of those 3 conditions was regarded as essential to any successful intervention in Indochina; and the Senators on this [Democratic] side of the aisle took the position that any intervention which occurred in the absence of meeting those conditions would be doomed to failure."

Kennedy warned on the Senate floor that day that colonialism would lead to future Vietnams. For this reason, he urged that the U.S. "emphasize the policy of independence for all peoples." "There is no doubt that we have paid a heavy price since 1945 in order to conciliate the British and the French," Kennedy declared. "We have paid a heavy price in connection with our relationship with the peoples of the Middle East and Asia. It seems to me we should realize what a heavy price we have paid, and in the future, we should emphasize the policy of independence for all peoples and equal opportunities for them to develop and maintain a policy of self-government. If we continue to pay the price, we are going to be faced with other Indochinas all over the world where colonialism is maintained."

Kennedy's next major statement on Vietnam was made June 1, 1956, when he addressed the "Conference of the American Friends of Vietnam" in Washington, D.C.

The American Friends of Vietnam had been founded in the fall of 1955. Its announced purpose was "to extend more broadly a mutual understanding of Vietnamese and American history, cultural customs and democratic institutions." In actuality, it was concerned with committing the U.S. to the support of what was fast becoming the *de facto* state of South Vietnam after that government indicated that it would not accept the nationwide elections provided for when the Geneva Accords, signed July 21, 1954, ended the war between France and the Viet Minh. The founding members of the American Friends of Vietnam included Sens. John Kennedy and Richard L. Neuberger (D., Ore.), Max Lerner, Arthur Schlesinger Jr. and Reps. Edna Kelly and Emmanuel Celler (both D., N.Y.).

The group was basically "liberal." It was convinced that communism could be thwarted by responsive, New Deal-like governments that could gain the confidence and support of people throughout the underdeveloped world. Kennedy told the Friends: "What we must offer [South Vietnam] ... is a revolution—a political and social revolution far superior to anything the Communists can offer."

In this June 1 speech Kennedy voiced "a plea that the United States never give its approval to the early nationwide elections called for by the Geneva Agreement of 1954. Neither the United States nor Free Vietnam was a party to that agreement—and neither the United States nor Free Vietnam is ever going to be a party to an election obviously stacked and subverted in advance, urged upon us by those who have broken their own pledges under the agreement they now seek to enforce."

Vietnam was of crucial strategic importance to the Free World, Kennedy said. "Let us briefly consider exactly what is 'America's stake in Vietnam'":

"*First,* Vietnam represents the cornerstone of the Free World in Southeast Asia, the keystone to the arch, the finger in the dike. Burma, Thailand, India, Japan, the Philippines and obviously Laos and Cambodia are among those whose security would be threatened if the red tide of communism overflowed into Vietnam. In the past, our policy-makers have sometimes issued contradictory statements on this point—but the long history of Chinese invasions of Southeast Asia being stopped by Vietnamese warriors should have removed all doubt on this subject. Moreover, the independence of free Vietnam is crucial to the Free World in fields other than the military. Her economy is essential to the economy of all of Southeast Asia; and her political liberty is an inspiration to those seeking to obtain or maintain their liberty in all parts of Asia—and indeed the world. The fundamental tenets of this nation's foreign policy, in short, depend in considerable measure upon a strong and free Vietnamese nation.

"*2d,* Vietnam represents a proving ground of democracy in Asia. However we may choose to ignore it or deprecate it, the rising prestige and influence of Communist China in Asia are unchallengeable facts. Vietnam represents the alternative to Communist dictatorship. If this democratic experiment fails, if some one million refugees have fled the totalitarianism of the North only to find neither freedom nor security in the South, then weakness, not strength, will characterize the meaning of democracy in the minds of still more Asians. The United States is directly responsible for this experiment—it is playing an important role in the laboratory where it is being conducted. We cannot afford to permit that experiment to fail.

"*3d,* and in somewhat similar fashion, Vietnam represents a test of American responsibility and determination in Asia. If we are not the parents of little Vietnam, then surely we are the godparents. We presided at its birth, we gave assistance to its life, we have helped to shape its future. As French influence in the political, economic and military spheres has declined in Vietnam, American influence has steadily grown. This is our offspring—we cannot abandon it, we cannot ignore its needs. And if it falls victim to any of the perils that threaten its existence—communism, political anarchy, poverty and the rest—then the United States, with some justification, will be held responsible; and our prestige in Asia will sink to a new low.

"4th and finally. America's stake in Vietnam, in her strength and in her security, is a very selfish one—for it can be measured, in the last analysis, in terms of American lives and American dollars. It is now well known that we were at one time on the brink of war in Indochina—a war which could well have been more costly, more exhausting and less conclusive than any war we have ever known. The threat of such war is not now altogether removed from the horizon. Military weakness, political instability or economic failure in the new state of Vietnam could change almost overnight the apparent security which has increasingly characterized that area under the leadership of Pres. [Ngo Dinh] Diem. And the key position of Vietnam in Southeast Asia, as already discussed, makes inevitable the involvement of this nation's security in any new outbreak of trouble.

"It is these 4 points, in my opinion, that represent America's stake in Vietnamese security...."

For the next 4 years while in the Senate, Kennedy said little about Vietnam. In 1959 he wrote an introduction and some commentary for a collection of his speeches that was being edited by Allan Nevins. The book was published in 1960 under the title *The Strategy of Peace.* Kennedy's attitude toward Vietnam at that time was one of ebullience. He wrote: Following the Geneva Conference, "in what everyone thought was the hour of total Communist triumph, we saw a near miracle take place. Despite the chaos, despite the universal doubts, a determined band of patriotic Vietnamese around one man of faith, Pres. [Ngo Dinh] Diem, began to release and to harness the latent power of nationalism to create an independent, anti-Communist Vietnam. Today that brave little state is working in friendly and free association with the United States, whose economic and military aid has, in conditions of independence, proved to be effective."

1960 Campaign

Satisfied with recent developments there, Kennedy said little more about Vietnam during his successful campaign for the Presidency in 1960.

On 3 occasions, however, Kennedy criticized the Republican nominee, Richard M. Nixon, for suggesting in 1954 that American troops be sent to Vietnam to aid the French. "If ever there was a war where we would have been engaged in a hopeless struggle without allies, for an unpopular colonialist cause, it was the 1954 war in Indochina," he said in a speech in New York Oct. 12, 1960. In a speech in Alexandria, Va. Aug. 24, Kennedy had criticized Nixon for having urged the French "to keep fighting" in Vietnam in 1954.

Kennedy appeared, during the campaign, to believe that North Vietnam was dominated by the Soviet Union. In Pikesville, Md. Sept. 16, he criticized the Soviet Communist Party leader Nikita Khrushchev for keeping an "iron empire... all the way from East Berlin to Vietnam."

Throughout the campaign Kennedy reiterated his long-held conviction that it was incumbent on the U.S. to associate itself with the underdeveloped world's longing for independence. In Salt Lake City Sept. 23 he said:

"If there is any lesson which the last 10 years has shown to me, and it is a lesson that I have been particularly interested in in Algeria and Indochina, it is that the strongest force in the world today is the desire to be independent. This is going to cause us all kinds of trouble in the next 10 years. People who used to support us will be neutral. But in the final analysis, it is our greatest source of strength. We desire to be independent; so do they. They desire to be independent of us. They desire to be independent of Western Europe, but they also desire to be independent of the Soviet Union and the Chinese Communists. We do not desire to dominate them. They do.

"Therefore, if we can associate ourselves with this great tide, and it has been a source of regret to me since the end of World War II that we have not associated ourselves with it, then I think we can move with history, and we can help form it and help shape it, and by the year 2000 the tide will have turned against the Communists and in the direction of freedom. We, in other words, fit in with the basic movement of our time. The Communists do not." If "we" succeed in this, "then our security and our leadership is assured."

U.S. involvement in Vietnam increased significantly in 1961, John Kennedy's first year as President. Shortly after his inauguration, Kennedy announced that U.S. combat forces would be especially trained and equipped to fight Communist revolutionaries. Later that year he warned that the "gates will open" should the Communists succeed in Indochina.

In May and again in October Kennedy acknowledged that he was considering sending U.S. combat troops to South Vietnam. Understandably reluctant to take this step, however, he decided instead to increase the number of U.S. military advisers in South Vietnam from approximately 800 to 16,000. By the end of the year U.S. helicopters were transporting South Vietnamese troops, and U.S. advisers, attached to South Vietnamese units were authorized to fire back if fired on.

Specialist 4th Class James T. Davis of Livingston, Tenn. was killed Dec. 21, 1961 when a truck in which he was riding with a detachment of South Vietnamese troops was ambushed by the Viet Cong 10 miles west of Saigon. He was the first American to die as part of the buildup ordered by Pres. Kennedy. 2 other Americans had been killed previously—in July 1959—by Communist gunfire in Vietnam since France had given up the fight there in 1954. By the end of 1962, American combat deaths in Vietnam climbed to 21, by the end of 1963 to 97 and by the end of 1964 to nearly 250.

Pres. Kennedy made 3 major decisions regarding Vietnam in 1961. He decided (a) to hold the line in South Vietnam in the face of heightened Communist guerrilla activity, (b) to increase the Eisenhower commitment and (c) to make the survival of the Saigon government a major objective of American foreign policy. According to some analysts, these decisions have been related to other events in 1961: the Bay of Pigs, the construction of the Berlin wall and a weakening of the American position in Laos coupled with Kennedy's determination to demonstrate the resolution of his new Administration.

Pledge to Defend Liberty, Warning Against Communism

In his first major pronouncements as President, Kennedy defined the U.S. role as a global defender of liberty. He warned that the major menace to liberty was communism.

Kennedy gave this pledge in his Inaugural Address Jan. 20, 1961: "Let every nation know, whether it wishes us well or ill, that we shall pay any price, bear any burden, meet any hardship, support any friend, oppose any foe, in order to assure the survival and the success of liberty."

17

In his first State-of-the-Union Message, delivered Jan. 30, Kennedy told Congress that "the tide of events has been running out and time has not been our friend" in various trouble spots throughout the world: In Asia "the relentless pressures of the Chinese Communists menace the security of the entire area—from the borders of India and South Vietnam to the jungles of Laos." "We must never be lulled into believing" that either Russia or China "has yielded its ambitions for world domination," he warned.

In an address before a group of newspaper editors in New York Apr. 20, Kennedy warned: "Too long we have fixed our eyes on traditional military needs, on armies prepared to cross borders, on missiles poised for flight. Now it should be clear that this is no longer enough—that our security may be lost piece by piece, country by country, without the firing of a single missile or the crossing of a single border." He pledged to train and equip the nation's armed forces to combat Communist revolutionaries.

At his press conference the following day, Kennedy predicted that guerrilla operations, such as those then under way in Vietnam, would occur in other parts of the world throughout the decade. That "seems to be one of the great problems now before the United States," he said.

Kennedy, speaking at a Democratic Party dinner in Chicago Apr. 28, said that in South Vietnam "a small army of guerrillas, organized and sustained by the Communist Viet Minh in the north, control most of the countryside in the nighttime—in the last 12 months have assassinated over 4,000 civil officers, 2,000 state employes and 2,000 police, believing if they can 'spill the wine,' that they can win control of the population." The U.S. was prepared to meet its obligations in Vietnam and the rest of the world "but we can only help those who are ready to bear their share of the burden themselves," he said.

Increased guerrilla activity in South Vietnam was reported by State Secy. Dean Rusk at his press conference in Washington May 4. According to Rusk, Viet Cong forces in South Vietnam had grown to 12,000 men and had killed or kidnaped more than 3,000 persons in 1960. Rusk declared that the U.S. would give South Vietnam "every possible help, across the entire spectrum in which help is needed." He refused, however, to say whether the U.S. would intervene militarily.

Chairman J. W. Fulbright (D., Ark.) of the Senate Foreign Relations Committee met with Kennedy later May 4 and told newsmen that he (Fulbright) would support the sending of U.S. combat troops to South Vietnam and Thailand if the Administration deemed necessary. Fulbright conceded that he had opposed U.S. military intervention in Laos, but he said the Laotians had shown indifference to their fate whereas the South Vietnamese and Thai had proved willing to defend themselves against communism.

JFK Considers Sending Troops to Vietnam

Kennedy indicated shortly thereafter that he was trying to decide whether to order American fighting men into the Vietnamese struggle. He announced May 5 that Vice Pres. Lyndon B. Johnson would go to Asia to help decide the nature and extent of U.S. aid needed by South Vietnam. The President said: "The problem of troops ... and the matter of what are we going to do to assist Vietnam obtain its independence is ... still under consideration."

Vice Pres. Johnson, accompanied by his wife and Jean and Stephen Smith, Pres. Kennedy's sister and brother-in-law, arrived in Saigon May 11, 1961. Addressing the South Vietnamese National Assembly May 12, Johnson declared that the U.S. was ready "immediately" to help expand South Vietnam's armed forces and to "meet the needs of your people on education, rural development, new industry and long-range economic development." Johnson met with Pres. Ngo Dinh Diem May 12. He said at a reception later that day that the U.S. was ready to stand "shoulder to shoulder" with South Vietnam in its war against communism, and he hailed Diem as the ("Winston Churchill of South Asia." An agreement for increased U.S. military and economic assistance for South Vietnam was made public in a joint communique issued in Saigon May 13 by Johnson and Diem. The aid increases were to be used primarily (a) to strengthen the South Vietnamese civil guard (40,000 men; 32,000 more in training) and army (150,000 men; 20,000 more requested), and (b) to support social welfare and public works programs.

Johnson flew to Manila May 13 and told a joint session of the Philippine Congress: "America will honor her commitments to the cause of freedom throughout the community of free nations"; "we will ... proceed either alone or with our free friends to preserve our position in Asia." Johnson flew to Bangkok, Thailand May 16, met privately several times with Field Marshal Sarit Thanarat May 16-18 and said at a Bangkok news conference May 17 that he had made it "abundantly clear" to Sarit that the U.S. would aid Thailand against any Communist pressure. The Vice President landed in Karachi May 20 on the final stop of his tour and conferred with Pakistani Pres. Mohammed Ayub Khan. In a speech at a Karachi civic reception, Johnson reiterated the U.S.' pledges of support for Asian efforts to combat "subversion, infiltration and terror."

Johnson returned to Washington May 24 and reported to Kennedy at the White House that "the battle against communism must be joined in Southeast Asia with strength and determination to achieve success there—or the United States inevitably must surrender the Pacific and take up our defenses on our own shores." The Vice President recommended that the U.S. "move forward promptly with a major effort to help these countries defend themselves." According to

Johnson: "The fundamental decision required of the United States—
and time is of the greatest importance—is whether we are to attempt
to meet the challenge of Communist expansion now in Southeast Asia
by a major effort in support of the forces of freedom in the area or
throw in the towel. The decision must be made in full realization of the
very heavy and continuing cost involved in terms of money, of effort
and of United States prestige. It must be made with the knowledge
that at some point we may be faced with the further decision of
whether we commit major United States forces to the area or cut our
losses and withdraw should our efforts fail. We must remain masters
of this decision."

Following his meeting with Kennedy, Johnson told newsmen that
his trip had convinced him that the U.S. must support efforts on a
"broad regional basis" to "banish the curse of poverty, illness and
illiteracy" in Asia. He declared that no country he visited had
requested U.S. troops and that the U.S. did not plan to send armed
forces to Asia.

Kennedy broke with tradition the next day by delivering in
person a "Special Message to the Congress on Urgent National
Needs." In the message he requested an additional $100 million in
Asian military and economic aid, the bulk to be allocated to South
Vietnam, Thailand and Pakistan.

De Gaulle's Warning Disregarded

Kennedy discussed the Indochina situation with French Pres.
Charles de Gaulle May 31, 1961 during a 3-day state visit to France. In
the first volume of his memoirs (*The Renewal,* published Oct. 7, 1970),
de Gaulle recalled warning Kennedy against letting the U.S. become
involved in the Vietnamese fighting.

De Gaulle reported telling Kennedy: "For you, intervention in
this region will be an entanglement without end. From the moment
that nations have awakened, no foreign authority, whatever its means,
has any chance of imposing itself on them. You are going to see this.
For, although you find officials who, by interest, agree to obey you,
the people will not consent and moreover are not calling for you. The
ideology that you invoke will not change anything. Even more, the
masses will confuse it with your will to exert power. This is why the
more you commit yourself there against communism, the more the
Communists will appear to be champions of national independence, the
more they will receive help and, first of all, that which comes from
desperation. We French have experienced this. You Americans
wanted, yesterday, to take our place in Indochina. You now want to
assume our succession to rekindle a war that we ended. I predict to you
that you will, step by step, become sucked into a bottomless military
and political quagmire despite the losses and expenditure that you may

squander. What you, we and others should do in this unfortunate Asia is not to substitute ourselves for states on their own soil but to give them what they need to get out of poverty and humiliation which are, there as elsewhere, the causes of totalitarian regimes. I say this to you in the name of our West."

In June, the U.S. took another step in its growing involvement in the fighting in Vietnam. Nguyen Dinh Thuan, the Diem cabinet's state secretary for the coordination of security matters, met with Kennedy June 14 to transmit a message from Diem requesting that U.S. military instructors be used to train South Vietnamese soldiers "directly" instead of training Vietnamese who in turn would serve as combat instructors. Thuan and U.S. officials reached agreement June 16 on a program for the direct training and combat supervision of Vietnamese by U.S. instructors.

The specific terms of the accord signed by Johnson and Diem in May were negotiated in South Vietnam in June and July by a 6-member economic survey committee headed by Dr. Eugene Staley of the Stanford (Calif.) Research Institute. The committee's work was the subject of a report submitted to Kennedy July 29. The report urged U.S. aid for a 15% increase in South Vietnam's armed forces, the resettlement of indefensible villages in 100 self-contained "agrovilles" and a long-range development program intended to improve the general economy and internal communications. Estimated cost of the program submitted to Kennedy: $50-$100 million.

Kennedy conferred with Nationalist Chinese officials at the White House July 31-Aug. 1. In a joint communique issued Aug. 2, Kennedy and Gen. Chen Cheng, Nationalist China's vice president and premier, noted that the U.S. was determined that South Vietnam "shall not be lost for lack of any [U.S.] support." Also at the talks was Foreign Min. Shen Chang-huan.

Bad News in Struggle Against Communists

Later in Aug. 1961 the journalist Theodore H. White informed the White House that the Communist guerrillas controlled almost all of the Mekong Delta, "so much so that I could find no American who would drive me outside Saigon in his car even by day without a military convoy." He reported a "political breakdown of formidable proportions": "What perplexes the hell out of me is that the Commies, on their side, seem to be able to find people willing to die for their cause.... I find it discouraging to spend a night in a Saigon nightclub full of young fellows of 20 to 25 dancing ... while 20 miles away their Communist contemporaries are terrorizing the countryside."

Pres. Kennedy told the UN General Assembly Sept. 25 that the world community faced 2 serious threats—Vietnam and Berlin. Kennedy, speaking at UN headquarters in New York, said: "The smoldering coals of war in Southeast Asia" are a "threat to the peace." "South Vietnam is already under attack.... The peaceful borders of Burma, Cambodia and India have been repeatedly violated." Laos was in danger of losing its independence. The "question confronting the world community is whether measures can be devised to protect the small and the weak from such tactics. For if they are successful in Laos and South Vietnam, the gates will be open."

The deterioration of the South Vietnamese military situation in the fall of 1961 brought new reports that the Kennedy Administration was considering U.S. intervention to prevent the Diem regime's over-throw. A State Department statement issued Oct. 2 said the U.S. was "pressing ahead with urgent measures to increase the ability of the South Vietnamese soldier to defend his country." It was reported that the Administration had decided to send U.S. combat and training formations to Communist-threatened areas of Southeast Asia if nec-essary. But State Department press officer Lincoln White told news-men Oct. 11 that "there has been no such decision. Furthermore,... Vietnam assures us...that with U.S. material assistance and training services, it can handle the present Communist aggressive attacks."

The U.S.' reported decision to intervene militarily was said to have been transmitted to other SEATO (South-East Asia Treaty Organization) nations at the 15th semi-annual meeting of the alliance's military advisers, held in Bangkok Oct. 3-6. A final communique issued by the advisers Oct. 6 said only that they had "decided upon practical measures to increase... the effectiveness of SEATO defenses to defeat any aggression."

Kennedy announced at his news conference in Washington Oct. 11 that he had directed retired Gen. Maxwell D. Taylor to "go to Saigon to discuss...ways in which we can perhaps better assist... Vietnam in meeting...[the] threat to its independence." Responding to reporters' queries on whether he was considering sending U.S. combat troops to South Vietnam, Thailand or Laos, Kennedy said that "we're going to wait till Gen. Taylor comes back" with information and "then we can come to conclusions." (In a personal message to Diem on South Vietnam's 6th independence day Oct. 26, Kennedy again pledged that "the United States is determined to help Vietnam preserve its independence, protect its people against Communist assassins and build a better life." Kennedy told Diem that he would be able to "consider with you additional measures that we might take to assist... Vietnam" after he received Taylor's report.)

Taylor flew to Saigon Oct. 18 accompanied by White House aide Walt W. Rostow. They met with Diem immediately after their arrival and consulted Oct. 19 with South Vietnamese army leaders and Lt. Gen. Lionel C. McGarr, head of the U.S. Military Advisory Group. Taylor flew Oct. 21 to Dongha, 450 miles north of Saigon on the border between North and South Vietnam, to inspect South Vietnamese units in the field; he conferred again with Diem in Dalat Oct. 21 and toured the Mekong River delta area by plane Oct. 22. Taylor conferred with U.S. officers in Saigon Oct. 23 and met again with Diem Oct. 24. Taylor, leaving for Thailand Oct. 25, urged in a farewell statement that South Vietnam begin a "national mobilization" in the "political, economic, military and psychological fields." He expressed "great confidence in the military capability of South Vietnam to cope with anything within its borders."

Taylor returned to Washington Nov. 3 and told newsmen that his report to the President would stress Diem's ability "to prevail against the Communist threat" to his country. He refused, however, to tell newsmen whether he would recommend sending U.S. combat forces to South Vietnam. In his report to Pres. Kennedy, Taylor described the situation in Vietnam as serious but not hopeless and recommended that American troops perform tasks in Vietnam—such as airlift and air reconnaissance—that the South Vietnamese were not prepared to handle. Taylor further envisaged sending some 10,000 American troops to Vietnam to guard against a conventional Korea-type attack from North Vietnam while the South Vietnamese dealt with the guerrillas to the rear. The Taylor report was not released to the public.

Kennedy was reported to be reluctant to send combat troops to Vietnam, preferring instead to aid the Diem regime with an infusion of American advisers. "They [Taylor and Rostow] want a force of American troops," he told White House aide Arthur M. Schlesinger Jr. later in Nov. 1961. "They say it's necessary in order to restore confidence and maintain morale. But it will be just like Berlin. The troops will march in; the bands will play; the crowds will cheer; and in 4 days everyone will have forgotten. Then we will be told we have to send in more troops. It's like taking a drink. The effect wears off, and you have to take another."

JFK Pledges More Aid

New requests from South Vietnam in Dec. 1961 brought a fresh Kennedy pledge of aid.

Pres. Diem wrote Pres. Kennedy Dec. 7 that "the forces of international communism now arrayed against us are more than we can meet with the resources at hand. We must have further assistance from the United States if we are to win the war now being waged against us," he said.

Kennedy replied by letter Dec. 14 that the U.S. was "prepared to help the Republic of Vietnam [South Vietnam] to protect its people and to preserve its independence" and that "we shall promptly increase our assistance to your defense effort...."

It was reported in Washington Dec. 16 that Diem had agreed to U.S. demands for a joint program to assess South Vietnam's need for rapid and radical reforms to assure economic and military efficiency. The reports, circulated by Kennedy Administration officials, came after intensive negotiations between Diem and U.S. Amb.-to-South Vietnam Frederick E. Nolting Jr. It had been reported from Saigon Nov. 26 that Diem had refused to accept U.S. demands that his regime be liberalized, but an agreement reportedly was reached after the U.S. threatened to recall Nolting and curtail its aid. In return for Diem's assent to the reforms, the U.S. was said to have promised a heavy increase in its economic and military aid programs, as indicated by Kennedy's Dec. 14 letter.

U.S. Military Personnel; Helicopters Arrive

The U.S. aircraft ferry-carrier *Core* arrived in Saigon Dec. 11, 1961 with 33 U.S. Army helicopters and 400 air and ground crewmen assigned to operate them for the South Vietnamese army. The helicopter consignment was the first overt indication of direct U.S. involvement in the war in South Vietnam. It followed an announcement by State Secy. Rusk Dec. 8 that the U.S. was consulting with its allies on the provision of joint economic and technical defense support for Vietnam. Rusk said that South Vietnam was in "clear and present danger" of Communist conquest and that guerrilla campaign in South Vietnam had approached the proportions of "conventional warfare."

The U.S. Military Assistance Advisory Group in Vietnam had been limited by the Geneva Accords of 1954 to a strength of 685 officers and men. Most were instructors in the use of arms and equipment supplied under U.S. aid programs. Other U.S. troops were in South Vietnam as guerrilla warfare instructors and specialists. It was reported Nov. 12 that 4 U.S. F-101 reconnaissance jets were engaged in the photo-spotting of guerrilla units in remote areas vulnerable only to air attack.

The *N.Y. Times* reported Dec. 20 that uniformed U.S. troops and specialists were "operating in battle areas with South Vietnamese forces" and, although not in combat, were authorized to fire back if fired on. The troops, said to number about 2,000, were described as operating aircraft and transport and communications facilities. The *Times* reported that the U.S. had delivered $500 million worth of military equipment to South Vietnam in the past 7 years, $65 million worth in 1961.

Saigon dispatches had reported Nov. 9 that Air Force Globemasters had begun transporting large amounts of equipment to South Vietnam from Clark Field in the Philippines. The equipment was said to be intended for a small force of B-26 bombers, fighters and helicopters scheduled to be given to South Vietnam together with services of 200 air and ground crew instructors.

GROWTH OF U.S. INVOLVEMENT: 1962

In 1962, for the 2d consecutive year, and amidst complaints that he was not being candid about the U.S. role in Vietnam, Pres. Kennedy increased the U.S. military involvement there. U.S. pilots began strafing enemy targets, and U.S. aircraft were used to carry South Vietnamese troops into combat. In the fall, U.S. helicopter crewmen began firing first on Viet Cong troops encountered during their missions with South Vietnamese forces.

Kennedy claimed in September that his Administration had succeeded in stopping the Communist move in Laos and South Vietnam. Sen. Mike Mansfield did not share that optimism, however.

U.S. Increases Military & Economic Aid

Asked at his press conference Jan. 2 if American troops were "now in combat in Vietnam," Kennedy answered, "No." But he soon made it clear that his Administration was increasing, and intended to increase the adoption of a broad spectrum of military and economic measures to help Saigon fight the Communists.

In his State of the Union Message, delivered Jan. 11, Kennedy told Congress that Vietnam was "where the foe is increasing his tactics of terror—where our own efforts have been stepped up—and where the local government has initiated new programs and reforms to broaden the base of resistance. The systematic aggression now bleeding that country is not a 'war of liberation'—for Vietnam is already free. It is a war of attempted subjugation—and it will be resisted."

The U.S. and South Vietnamese governments announced Jan. 4 that they would cooperate in starting "a broad economic and social program aimed at providing every Vietnamese with the means for improving his standard of living." The program was planned as part of the Kennedy Administration's efforts to strengthen South Vietnam against the Viet Cong. The U.S. had exerted pressure on the Diem government to institute reforms designed to enable it to combat the Communist rebels effectively in the social and economic as well as the military field. Diem had resisted most of the suggested political reforms. The program was to be financed by South Vietnam through heavy duties on luxury imports and a new tax system. The U.S. would provide advice, support essential imports and finance specific projects. State Department officials said U.S. expenditures for South Vietnam would rise "appreciably" above the $136 million worth of economic aid provided in 1961. The announcement stressed that the U.S. "simultaneously" would act to strengthen South Vietnam militarily "pursuant" to the Dec. 1961 exchange of letters between Pres. Kennedy and Pres. Diem.

At his press conference Jan. 31, Kennedy described the situation in Vietnam as "one that's of great concern to us," and he reiterated that the U.S. "has increased its help to the government [of South Vietnam]." The situation in Vietnam was "extremely serious," he said, and he cited nearly 500 Communist-inspired incidents during the past week. "I'm hopeful," he said, "that the [International] Control Commission will continue to examine" the situation "and come to some conclusions in regard to the Geneva Accords."

In a Voice of America broadcast to South Vietnam on the Vietnamese New Year, Kennedy declared Feb. 5: "In your struggle against the aggressive forces of communism, the sacrifices that you have willingly made, the courage you have shown, the burdens you have endured have been a source of inspiration to people all over the world. Let me assure you of our continued assistance in the development of your capabilities to maintain your freedom and to defeat those who wish to destroy that freedom."

As evidence of the Kennedy Administration's determination to aid Saigon, dispatches from the fighting area told of continued involvement of U.S.-manned helicopters. South Vietnamese troops recaptured the guerrilla-held village of Hungmy Feb. 4 in a surprise airborne attack mounted with U.S. helicopters and crews. A helicopter was shot down in the operation, but its crew was saved, and the craft later was repaired and flown out. 15 helicopters were used in the attack; they first shuttled troops to an assembly point near the village, then flew them directly into the village, behind the guerrillas' positions. Officials conceded, however, that the attack had failed in that 130 Viet Cong guerrillas had escaped and only 3 were captured. (Hungmy was situated at South Vietnam's extreme southern tip.) A 2d U.S. helicopter was shot down and crashed without loss of life Feb. 6 in a similar raid.

Political Dispute Over U.S. Involvement

As the Kennedy Administration continued to send increasing numbers of armed and uniformed Americans to Vietnam during 1962, the President and his advisers found themselves engaged in a growing political controversy over the extent to which the U.S. was becoming embroiled in the fighting there.

At his Feb. 7 news conference, Kennedy was asked how deeply the U.S. was involved in South Vietnam and whether the American people had the right to know what their forces were doing in what seemed to be a growing war. The President answered: "We are out there on training and on transportation, and we are assisting, in every way we properly can, the people of South Vietnam who with the greatest courage and under danger are attempting to maintain their freedom. Now this is an area where there is a good deal of danger, and it's a matter of information. We don't want to have [publicize] information which is of assistance to the enemy—and it is a matter I think will have to be worked out with the government of Vietnam, which bears the primary responsibility."

The Republican National Committee's publication *Battle Line* charged in its Feb. 13 issue that Kennedy had been "less than candid" about U.S. involvement in the Vietnam fighting. The bulletin called on Kennedy to "make a full report" on the extent of this intervention. It said: The U.S. should be informed if it was "moving toward another Korea"; "the people should not have to wait until American casualty lists are posted"; "we would ask Pres. Kennedy if it isn't time to drop the pretense that the United States is merely acting as military adviser to South Vietnam."

Asst. State Secy. W. Averell Harriman told the Senate Foreign Relations Committee Feb. 13 that the Kennedy Administration had "no present plans for commitment of American combat forces" in the Vietnamese fighting.

Kennedy said at his Feb. 14 news conference that all major U.S. moves to support the South Vietnamese government had the approval of "a very strong bipartisan concensus" of Republicans and Democrats. He advised that "the headquarters of both our parties should ... leave these matters to be discussed by responsible leaders on both sides." He said he had been as "frank" as possible, "consistent" with "security," on the nature of the U.S.' involvement in Vietnam. He reiterated that "the training missions that we have there have been instructed that if they are fired upon, they are of course to fire back, but we have not sent combat troops in [the] generally understood sense of the word."

Commenting on charges that Kennedy had concealed the extent of the U.S. involvement, ex-Vice Pres. Richard M. Nixon said Feb. 15: "I don't agree at all with any partisan or other criticism of the U.S. build-up in Vietnam. My only question is whether it may be too little and too late.... I support Pres. Kennedy to the hilt, and I only hope he will step up the build-up and under no circumstances curtail it because of possible criticism."

Dispute over the Kennedy Administration's credibility regarding Vietnam was exacerbated by a directive sent by the State Department Feb. 21 to U.S. officials in South Vietnam. The directive, concerning relations with the U.S. press, was referred to as Cable No. 1006 and was classified, but a copy was shown to members of the House Subcommittee on Foreign Operations & Government Information, headed by Rep. John E. Moss, (D., Calif.). The subcommittee's report of Oct. 1, 1963 paraphrased the cable as saying:

● News stories criticizing the Diem government "increase the difficulties of the U.S. job."

● Newsmen "should be advised that trifling or thoughtless criticism of the Diem government would make it difficult to maintain co-operation" with Diem.

● Newsmen "should not be transported on military activities of the type that are likely to result in undesirable stories."

Ex-White House Press Secy. Pierre Salinger has reported in his book *With Kennedy* that the cable "was shown to both Pres. Kennedy and his national security adviser, McGeorge Bundy, before being sent to the field."

The subcommittee said in its report (Oct. 1963): "The restrictive U.S. press policy in Vietnam ... unquestionably contributed to the lack of information about conditions in Vietnam, which created an international crisis. Instead of hiding the facts from the American public, the State Department should have done everything possible to expose the full situation to full view."

At his press conference Mar. 7, Kennedy was told that, whereas there had been a scattering of very favorable news stories out of South Vietnam, it was, nevertheless, difficult for the press to report on the war because the Pentagon "won't put out anything." Asked to comment, Kennedy replied: "I'm not familiar with it, and it's a matter, really, I think, of the Defense Department, but it has not come to me. In any case, it's a matter, really, for the Vietnamese."

U.S. Forms Vietnam Command

The Defense Department announced Feb. 8, 1962 that a new U.S. military command was being formed in South Vietnam to coordinate all U.S. military support for the Diem government. The new unit, the U.S. Military Assistance Command (MAC), Vietnam, was to be commanded by Gen. Paul D. Harkins, former U.S. Army deputy commander-in-chief in the Pacific. A Pentagon spokesman said Feb. 9 that the new command was a demonstration of the Kennedy Administration's belief that "this is a war we can't afford to lose" and that "we're drawing a line" against Communist subversion in South Vietnam.

State Secy. Rusk said at a Washington news conference Mar. 1 that the Vietnamese war could be ended easily if the Communist nations halted their intervention and encouragement of the Viet Cong. Although he declared that the U.S. was always ready to discuss peace, he expressed doubt that it would be useful to convene international talks on Vietnam, as proposed by the Soviet bloc. Rusk said: "There can be peace overnight in Vietnam if those responsible for the aggression wish peace. It is as simple as that."

Dissidents Bomb Diem's Palace

The South Vietnamese presidential palace in Saigon was bombed and partially burned Feb. 27 (Feb. 26 U.S. time) by 2 dissident South Vietnamese air force pilots flying U.S.-supplied AD-6 fighter-bombers. Pres. Ngo Dinh Diem was in the palace when the planes attacked but was not injured. Mr. and Mrs. Ngo Dinh Nhu, the president's influential brother and sister-in-law, also in the palace, were unhurt except for minor injuries to Mrs. Nhu when she fell during the raid. The only person known to have been killed during the raid was Sidney Ambrose, 49, an American technician, who fell from a roof while watching the attack. In a personal message cabled to Diem Feb. 27, Pres. Kennedy said he was "very gratified to learn that you are safe ... and wish to express my admiration for the calm and courageous manner in which you faced this destructive and vicious act."

Thereafter, Diem denied his air force any more 500-pound bombs. He had banned all significant troop movements without his personal approval after an attempted *coup d'etat* in 1960.

The *N.Y. Times* reported Mar. 13 that Phan Huy Quat, president of South Vietnam's opposition Committee on National Union, had appealed to U.S. Amb.-to-Saigon Frederick Nolting Jr. to intercede for liberalization of the Diem government. Quat reportedly contended that many Vietnamese nationalists and the bulk of South Vietnam's population had been alienated from the regime by its suppression of political and civil rights. He appealed to Nolting to urge that non-Communist opposition leaders be freed from jail and that loyal nationalist groups be permitted to present their grievances. Nolting had told South Vietnamese in a Saigon speech Feb. 15 that "my government fully supports your elected constitutional government" despite the criticism of the Diem regime by what he called misguided "skeptics." Nolting conceded that there had been delay in carrying out promised reforms and local aid programs, but he declared that the only hope for success against the Viet Cong lay with "the dedicated and courageous leadership of your president."

(Stanley Millet, a U.S. professor who had spent a year in South Vietnam, reported in *Harper's* in September: "In that entire year I never heard a single Vietnamese voice raised in defense of the Diem regime. High and low, government officials, professors, army officers and students condemned it and yearned for a change—a *coup d'etat* which would rid them of Diem before the Communists crushed him.")

Americans Join Fighting

U.S. State Department officials confirmed Mar. 9, 1962 that American pilots were flying combat-training missions with South Vietnamese airmen over guerrilla-held areas of South Vietnam. They would neither confirm nor deny that these missions involved bombing and strafing attacks on Viet Cong strongholds. Saigon dispatches of the UPI and Reuters had reported earlier Mar. 9 that the U.S. pilots were involved directly in attacks and that in most cases the Vietnamese airmen flew as co-pilots. The UPI said that such use of U.S. pilots had been going on for 2 months and that it had been justified as an emergency measure pending the training of combat-ready South Vietnamese airmen. *The Wall St. Journal* reported from Saigon Mar. 6 that the U.S. Army helicopters used to ferry South Vietnamese troops on raids against the guerrillas usually had American crewmen manning machineguns to return ground fire.

Additional instances of Kennedy Administration intervention in the Vietnamese fighting were reported by Western newsmen. According to these reports, U.S. personnel were taking a direct part in most major South Vietnamese combat actions. Among examples of such U.S. involvement:

● U.S. helicopters flew troops to besieged villages in Tay, Ninh and Phuoc Thanh Provinces Mar. 4, and Viet Cong units were forced to retreat after losing 110 killed in the 2 battles.

● The civil guard post of Botuc, near the Cambodian frontier, was rescued Mar. 4 when South Vietnamese planes strafed 500 guerrilla attackers and U.S. planes dropped 500 parachute troops with their American advisers. The guerrillas were said to have escaped, leaving 56 dead.

● South Vietnamese troops were flown by U.S. helicopters into an attack Mar. 6 on Viet Cong-held Caingai village, at the southern tip of the country. At least 25 guerrillas were killed in the action and accompanying strafing, but the bulk of the Communist force escaped. 5 helicopters were hit by ground fire; one was brought down but later was repaired and flown out.

● U.S. helicopters airlifted a battalion of South Vietnamese troops into action Mar. 13 against a force of 500 guerrillas operating along the upper Mekong River in Kien Hoa Province. It was reported Mar. 14, however, that the main body of guerrillas had escaped.

15 H-34 combat helicopters of the U.S.' 362d Marine Medium Helicopter Squadron landed in South Vietnam Apr. 15 from the aircraft carrier *Princeton*. The Marine helicopters, later based near Soctrang, capital of Ba Xuyen Province, 100 miles southwest of Saigon, reinforced the 3 U.S. Army helicopter companies already in South Vietnam. They were the first Marine air units sent to Vietnam.

Pres. Kennedy had said at his news conference in Washington Mar. 14 that while "a good many Americans" were serving in Vietnam, none could properly be termed "combat troops." He added that "if there were a basic change in that situation in Vietnam which calls for a constitutional decision [on whether to send troops], I ... would go to the Congress."

Defense Secy. Robert S. McNamara confirmed at a Washington news conference Mar. 15 that American servicemen in South Vietnam had exchanged fire with Communist guerrillas. McNamara was the first high-ranking Kennedy Administration official to confirm the reports that U.S. troops had been involved directly in the fighting. He said: "I think our mission in South Vietnam is very clear. We are there

at the request of the South Vietnamese government to provide training.... There has been sporadic fire aimed at United States personnel,
and in some minor instances they've had to return that fire." U.S.
advisers had taken part in "combat-type training missions" with
Vietnamese troops, but "Americans are under instructions not to fire
unless fired upon."

(McNamara left Washington for Honolulu Mar. 20, accompanied
by Adm. Harry D. Felt, U.S. Pacific commander, for his 3d Hawaiian
meeting of 1962 on the South Vietnamese situation. Returning from
these talks, McNamara told newsmen in San Francisco Mar. 22 that
U.S. assistance had enabled the South Vietnamese to take the offensive. McNamara, accompanied by Gen. Lyman L. Lemnitzer,
chairman of the Joint Chiefs of Staff, arrived in Saigon May 9 to
confer with U.S. and South Vietnamese officials, reportedly in an
effort to eliminate friction between them and to encourage Pres.
Diem's regime to a more effective prosecution of the war. McNamara
told newsmen that "there is no plan for introducing [American] combat
forces in South Vietnam." He toured South Vietnamese battle areas by
plane and helicopter May 9-10 and met with Diem late May 10 for a
strategy discussion attended by Adm. Felt and Gen. Harkins. He left
for Washington May 11 after saying at a Saigon news conference that
he was "tremendously encouraged" by developments in South Vietnam
and that he saw no reason for a large scale increase in U.S. military
aid to the Diem government.)

Kennedy, at his news conference Apr. 11, expressed concern
about the hazardous nature of duty in Vietnam for American troops
but added that we "cannot desist in Vietnam."

State Undersecy. George W. Ball warned Apr. 30 that the South
Vietnamese war would be a "slow, arduous" struggle of the sort not
liked by Americans. Addressing the Detroit Economic Club, Ball
asserted, however, that the war could be won if the U.S. maintained its
support for the South Vietnamese government and made possible the
defeat of the guerrillas by arms and attrition.

A report of the International Control Commission (ICC) for
Vietnam, made public May 25, condemned (a) North Vietnam for violating the Geneva Accords by fostering "subversion and aggression"
in South Vietnam, (b) the U.S. for violating the Accords with its
military buildup in South Vietnam, and (c) South Vietnam for violating the Accords by accepting U.S. military aid and establishing "a
factual military alliance" with the U.S.

JFK Sees Challenge to Freedom

Kennedy described the war in Indochina to the West Point
graduating class June 6 as "another type of war, new in its intensity
[but] ancient in its origin." Guerrilla wars constituted "the kinds of

challenges that will be before us in the next decade if freedom is to be
saved," he said.

In a fresh statement supporting "domino theory" views, Kennedy
claimed at his press conference June 14 that "a withdrawal in the case
of Vietnam and in the case of Thailand might mean a collapse of the
entire area."

U.S. Involvement Increases

Reports of U.S. participation in the Vietnamese fighting
mounted during the spring and summer of 1962.

U.S. Army and Marine helicopters flew South Vietnamese troops
into the Plaine des Joncs (Plain of Reeds) area in the Mekong River
delta May 2 and 6 in surprise raids on Viet Cong forces. 10 guerrillas
were reported killed May 2 and 57 killed May 6.

More than 1,000 South Vietnamese troops—flown into the area
by U.S. helicopters—engaged in 5 separate clashes with the Viet Cong
May 12 in one of the year's biggest battles in the Mekong delta about
75 miles southwest of Saigon. 2 helicopters were shot down but re-
covered. U.S. Col. Frank Butner Clay, senior adviser to the South
Vietnamese 7th Division, derided early reports that 300 guerrillas had
been killed; he said he doubted that more than 20 had been slain.

At least 4 U.S. servicemen acting in technical or advisory
capacities with South Vietnamese forces were killed in fighting with
guerrillas in June and July. 4 more Americans were reported killed or
missing July 15 in the crash of a U.S. Army helicopter shot down by
guerrillas. An unidentified U.S. pilot was killed July 16 in the crash of
a South Vietnamese Air Force C-47 near Kontum, in the central highlands; 22 Vietnamese also died in the crash.

The fighting grew in intensity during June, July and August, and
thousands of South Vietnamese troops were air-lifted aboard U.S.
military helicopters into hundreds of engagements against Viet Cong
guerrillas.

Some 4,000 South Vietnamese ground, air and naval troops, supported by U.S. planes, undertook a 16-day campaign against the Viet
Cong in the Camau Peninsula Aug. 15-30. The South Vietnamese
army reported Aug. 31 that 499 guerrillas had been killed in the drive.

The South Vietnamese government said Sept. 10 that its forces,
supported by U.S. helicopters, had killed 40 guerrillas, wounded 7 and
captured 4 in fighting that day in Kien Phong Province, 80 miles west
of Saigon.

Some 2,500 South Vietnamese soldiers, supported by U.S. heli-
copters, fighter-bombers and amphibious forces, killed at least 153
Viet Cong Sept. 18 in fighting around the Plaine des Joncs village of
Anhu, according to a report received by U.S. newsmen.

Long War Seen, Diem's Effectiveness Questioned

In Honolulu July 23 for a new round of talks on South Vietnam, Defense Secy. McNamara said that the war against the Viet Cong would be long and costly but could be won if the U.S. maintained its support of the Diem government. "It will take years rather than months," he said, "but the Communists eventually will be defeated." (McNamara had said at a Washington news conference July 6 that "we can't expect termination of a war ... [in] months. It will be years before it is concluded....") On leaving Honolulu July 24, he declared that the South Vietnamese were "beginning to hit the Viet Cong insurgents where it hurts most—in winning the people to the side of the government."

Gen. Maxwell D. Taylor, newly designated chairman of the U.S. Joint Chiefs of Staff, returned to South Vietnam Sept. 10-13 for talks with Diem and the commanders of the U.S. military assistance operations and to tour Vietnamese battle areas. Taylor, at a Saigon news conference Sept. 13, lauded the "resistance of the Vietnamese people to the subversive insurgency threat" and praised their "great national movement, assisted to some extent ... by Americans." Replying to reporters' questions of his view of the Diem regime's apparent lack of popularity, Taylor declared that once the "strategic hamlets" program was effective and the South Vietnamese could be assured protection against the Viet Cong, then "I believe the emphasis will shift from military more to economic and social activities."

"Guarded optimism" about the eventual outcome of the Vietnamese war was expressed by Roger Hilsman Jr., director of State Department intelligence and research, in an address in Chicago Sept. 18. Hilsman, a guerrilla warfare officer during World War II, asserted that the U.S.' "vigorous" support had given the South Vietnamese "new confidence." He said: (a) More than 2,000 "strategic hamlets," 1,000 of them radio-equipped, had been created. (b) None of the hamlets had "gone over" to the Viet Cong or had sold their arms to the guerrillas; all had "fought well," and only 5% had lost their radios to the Viet Cong. (c) In one week in August, "over 600 Viet Cong were killed as against less than 100 killed among the pro-government forces," and 2/3 of the Communists' casualties were inflicted by village defense units. (d) The Viet Cong's defection rates had gone up while the guerrilla recruitment program had faltered.

U.S. Helicopter Crews 'Fire First'

American helicopter crewmen were reported Oct. 15 to have begun to fire first on any Viet Cong formations encountered during their missions with South Vietnamese troops. The "fire-first" actions were attributed to crews of heavily armed Bell HU-IA helicopters in use for the first time as escorts for troop-carrying helicopters. The reports were repeated from Saigon despite a Defense Department statement in Washington that there had been no alteration of orders limiting U.S. personnel to shooting back if fired upon. Other dispatches confirmed the increasing role that U.S. helicopters and military advisers were playing in the fighting in 1962:

● The AP reported Oct. 15 that 3 HU-IAs—each of which carried 2 heavy machineguns and 16 rockets—had carried out an offensive strike against a Viet Cong stronghold in a mountainous area 55 miles northwest of Saigon. Although crewmen of the H-21 troop-carrying helicopters used in Vietnam already had exchanged fire with the guerrillas, they had observed the "return fire" orders and had been limited by their light armaments and their machines' vulnerability.

● 15 of the turbine-powered HU-IAs reportedly were in Vietnam; they were flown by U.S. Army crews but carried no national insignia.

● 7 Americans were killed Oct. 6 when their Marine H-34 helicopter crashed in a mountainous area near Quangngai, 330 miles north of Saigon. An unidentified U.S. soldier was killed Oct. 6 during a helicopter-borne raid in Dinh Tuong Province, south of Saigon. 3 Americans were killed Oct. 15 when their L-28 observation plane was shot down by Communist ground fire near Banmethuot in the central highlands.

● It was reported from Saigon Oct. 19 that Operation Morning Star, a major South Vietnamese effort to clear Tayninh Province, north of Saigon near the Cambodian border, had ended in relative failure. More than 5,000 South Vietnamese troops were said to have been ferried into action for 8 days by U.S. helicopters but were said to have killed only 40 Viet Cong troops and to have captured only 2 others. 25 more guerrillas were said to have been killed by fire from HU-IA attack helicopters, one of which was lost during the operation. U.S. officials termed the operation a waste of manpower and disclaimed responsibility for it.

● South Vietnamese troops launched a 4-day attack Nov. 1 near Vinh Long in the Mekong delta. 12 U.S. troop-carrying H-21 helicopters, 5 rocket-armed HU-IA escort helicopters and 600 South Vietnamese infantrymen were involved. South Vietnamese government sources estimated enemy losses as possibly as high as 250.

● U.S. military sources reported 64 Viet Cong killed Nov. 7 and 8 in the Plaine des Joncs, where 2 battalions of government troops were flown into battle by U.S. helicopters.

● Operation An Lac (Peace & Goodwill), a major drive to gain control of the Darlac Province highland area in central South Vietnam, was launched in November by U.S. advisers and South Vietnamese forces with these reported aims: (a) to isolate the Viet Cong in the south; (b) to harass guerrillas in the region until they were on the defensive; (c) to win over the primitive mountain tribesmen *(montagnards)*. The operation was scheduled to last 4 months and had been allocated more than a regiment of government troops. (Failure of the program was indicated by the South Vietnamese government's admission Dec. 20 that the Viet Cong had opened a new offensive in the region.)

● The most ambitious South Vietnamese effort to penetrate the guerrilla-held "D Zone," main Communist rest and supply area, was launched Nov. 20, when 800 troops were air-lifted into the region by 56 U.S.-piloted helicopters. Although 5,000 Viet Cong troops were believed to be in the area, 9 days of the top secret operation resulted only in 2 guerrilla deaths (the Saigon government gave the figure as 10). At least 4 South Vietnamese paratroopers were killed and 20 injured during jumps. The campaign was planned to last 3 weeks, but participating units were reassigned by Dec. 4. The operation involved up to 2,000 men.

JFK Lauds U.S. Efforts in Vietnam

In remarks by telephone to the Ohio Democratic Convention in Columbus Sept. 21, Pres. Kennedy had asserted that when his administration took office in 1961, "the Communists were on the move in Laos and South Vietnam. [But] in the months since, that tide has been reversed."

In a political speech in St. Paul, Minn. Oct. 6 Kennedy reported that the U.S. "has 7,000 Americans scattered over Vietnam participating in a guerrilla struggle." In Indianapolis Oct. 13 he said that his Administration, "recognizing the time had come to stop the decline in Southeast Asia, ... [had] committed 15 times as many men to the defense of that area [as had the previous administration]."

At his press conference Dec. 12, Kennedy noted that the U.S. "was putting on a major effort in Vietnam" and that "we have about 10 or 11 times as many men there as we had a year ago." The U.S. had suffered some casualties, he conceded, but in "some phases, the military program has been quite successful," he declared. He reported that the U.S. had shipped a great deal of equipment to South Vietnam and that "we are going ahead with the 'strategic hamlet' program."

Kennedy told the Economic Club of New York Dec. 14 that South Vietnam "would collapse instantaneously if it were not for the United States."

But in Saigon Dec. 2 Sen. Mike Mansfield (D., Mont.) became the first major U.S. official to refuse to make an optimistic public comment on the progress of the civil war. In South Vietnam as Kennedy's personal representative, the Senate majority leader rejected an "encouraging" departure statement prepared by the embassy and limited his comment to praise of Diem's personal integrity.

POLITICAL & MILITARY ENTANGLEMENT: 1963

In 1963 the Kennedy Administration reached the painful conclusion that the war could not be won unless the Diem regime were broadened and liberalized—or replaced by a reform-minded government. This finding, arrived at in the fall of 1963, resulted in Pres. Kennedy's decision to curtail certain economic aid to the Diem regime. The U.S.' open hostility towards Diem encouraged a clique of South Vietnamese generals to overthrow—and murder—Diem Nov. 1, 3 weeks before Kennedy's own assassination. Throughout the year, Kennedy underscored what he considered the strategic importance of South Vietnam and his acceptance of the so-called domino theory.

Senators Question U.S. Support

A U.S. Senate report Feb. 24 questioned the current high level of the Kennedy Administration's military and economic aid to the South Vietnamese government. In the report 4 Senators, suggesting that South Vietnam expend "further effort" in its struggle for "survival," declared that "there is no interest of the United States in Vietnam which would justify, in present circumstances, the conversion of the war ... primarily into an American war to be fought primarily with American lives." The report, submitted to the Senate Foreign Relations Committee by a 4-man panel headed by Senate majority leader Mike Mansfield (D., Mont.), was the result of an investigation of the U.S. aid program in Southeast Asia requested by Pres. Kennedy in 1962. The other subcommittee members were Sens. J. Caleb Boggs (R., Del.), Claiborne Pell (D., R.I.) and Benjamin A. Smith (D., Mass.).

The report also dealt with the U.S. aid program in Laos, Cambodia, Thailand, Burma and the Philippines. In submitting the subcommittee's findings to Sen. J. W. Fulbright (D., Ark.), committee chairman, Mansfield said emphasis had been placed on South Vietnam because the U.S.' greatest effort in Southeast Asia was centered in that country: an annual aid expenditure of $400 million and the stationing of 12,000 Americans there "on dangerous assignment." The report said:

● The U.S. should thoroughly reassess its "over-all security requirement on the Southeast Asia mainland" with a view to carrying out an orderly reduction in the U.S. aid programs. But "extreme caution" should be used in reducing such aid, "for if the attempt is made to alter the programs via a Congressional meat-axe cut ..., it runs the risk of not merely removing the fat but of leaving a gap which will lay open the region to massive chaos and, hence, jeopardize the present pacific structure of our national security."

● "Although not intended for combat," U.S. soldiers "have been in combat. More than 50 men have lost their lives—about 1/2 in battle—in Vietnam" since "the program of intensified assistance" began in 1961.

● The subcommittee, while deploring the size of U.S. aid needed to help the Vietnamese defeat the Viet Cong, conceded that it would be risky to reduce such aid.

37

● "In the very best of circumstances outside aid in very substantial size will be necessary for many years," even after Saigon forces defeated the Viet Cong.
● The "intensification [of U.S. aid] has carried us to the start of the road which leads to the point at which the conflict could become of greater concern and ... responsibility to the U.S. than it is to the government and people of South Vietnam."

Mansfield, recalling his visit to South Vietnam in 1955, said: "What is most disturbing is that Vietnam now appears to be, as it was then, only at the beginning of coping with its grave inner problems. All of the current difficulties existed in 1955, along with the hope and energy to meet them. But it is 7 years later and $2 billion of U.S. aid later. Yet, substantially the same difficulties remain, if, indeed they have not been compounded."

Kennedy, asked to comment on the Mansfield report, said at his press conference Mar. 6 that he did not "see how we are going to be able—unless we are going to pull out of Southeast Asia and turn it over to the Communists—how we are going to be able to reduce very much our economic programs and military programs in South Vietnam, in Cambodia, in Thailand. I think that unless you want to withdraw from the field and decided that it is in the national interest to permit that area to collapse, I would think that it would be impossible to substantially change it, particularly as we are in a very intensive struggle in those areas. So I think we ought to judge the economic burden it places upon us as opposed to having the Communists control all of Southeast Asia with the inevitable effect that this would have on the security of India and, therefore, really begin to—perhaps all the way toward the Middle East. So I think that while we would all like to lighten the burden, I don't see any real prospect of the burden being lightened for the U.S. in Southeast Asia in the next year if we are going to do the job and meet what I think are very clear national needs."

JFK Again Defends 'Domino Theory'

Kennedy, asked Apr. 24 at his press conference whether or not he subscribed to the so-called "falling domino" theory in Southeast Asia, Kennedy replied in the affirmative. "If Laos fell into Communist hands," he declared, "it would increase the danger along the northern frontiers of Thailand ... [and] would put additional pressure on South Vietnam, which in itself would put additional pressure on Malaya. So I do accept the view that there is an interrelationship in these countries and that is one of the reasons why we are concerned with maintaining the Geneva Accords as a method of maintaining stability in Southeast Asia."

In a "Special Message to the Congress on Free World Defense and Assistance Programs," Kennedy asserted Apr. 2 that "free Asia is responding resolutely to the political, economic and military challenge of Communist China's relentless efforts to dominate the continent."

Kennedy had claimed Jan. 14 in his State-of-the-Union message that the "spearpoint of aggression has been blunted in Vietnam." At that time the Viet Cong appeared somewhat shaken by the introduction of U.S. troop-carrying helicopters. 5 months later Kennedy was less optimistic. At his press conference May 22 he said that "as of today," he hoped to be able to begin withdrawing some U.S. troops from South Vietnam by the end of the year. But he said he couldn't make a final judgment until he had seen "the course of the struggle the next few months." Asked about a statement by Pres. Diem's brother, Ngo Dinh Nhu, that there were too many American troops in South Vietnam, Kennedy insisted that the U.S. "would withdraw the troops, any number of troops, anytime the government of South Vietnam would suggest it."

Communists Charge U.S. Uses Gas

The Soviet military newspaper *Krasnaya Zvezda (Red Star)* charged Mar. 9 that U.S. "interventionists" in South Vietnam had used "asphyxiation gases" and "noxious chemicals" in fighting the Viet Cong. The newspaper said that "hundreds of people perished, great quantities of cattle were poisoned."

Peking radio charged Mar. 9 that the U.S. had sprayed chemicals "to poison innocent South Vietnamese people and devastate crops." The broadcast said that 5,000 persons had been poisoned and that public meetings had been held in Hanoi "to censure the atrocities." Peking radio said the Chinese Red Cross had protested the use of "chemical poisons by U.S. imperialism to murder civilians and destroy crops in South Vietnam."

The Communist charges apparently referred to a tactic of spraying a weed killer from U.S. planes to destroy heavy foliage used as hiding places by the Viet Cong.

The U.S. State Department said Mar. 9: "We have never used poison gas in South Vietnam, and there is no truth in Communist reports that we are using it now"; the chemicals employed by U.S. pilots were "non-toxic to humans and animals when used in the prescribed manner, that is, sprayed on trees and underbrush in the open air."

Buddhist Unrest Shakes Diem Regime

Thousands of South Vietnam's Buddhists, led by their *bonzes* (priests) and nuns, took to the streets during 1963 in angry demonstrations against the government of Pres. Diem and his Roman Catholic family. The demonstrations were met by force. Police and troops fired on marchers, killing several persons and creating the first martyrs of a protest movement that was to become increasingly political in its aims. To these deaths were added those of a number of Buddhist priests and nuns who soaked their robes in gasoline and publicly burned themselves to death in protest against the repression of the Diem regime.

Pres. Kennedy, at his news conference July 17, acknowledged that the Buddhist dispute was hindering South Vietnam's war against the Viet Cong. He said, however, that the U.S. would not withdraw its military support from South Vietnam since "it would mean a collapse not only of South Vietnam but Southeast Asia."

In an action that brought an immediate U.S. denunciation of the Diem regime, Saigon authorities struck back at the Buddhist protest movement Aug. 21. Charging that Buddhist leaders were acting as tools of the Communists, the regime used military force to seize and occupy the country's major pagodas and arrest large numbers of priests and student demonstrators. The government's action precipitated a crisis in its relations with the U.S., which considered the repressive tactics unacceptable and a hindrance to the war against the Viet Cong. Diem imposed nationwide martial law later Aug. 21 amid reports that a military coup was about to be launched against his government.

The U.S. State Department Aug. 21 denounced the armed action against the Buddhists as a reversal of the Diem government's promise to the U.S. to reconcile its differences with the Buddhists. The department deplored what it said were repressive measures taken against Buddhist leaders.

U.S. Sounded Out on Plan for Coup

The U.S. attack on Diem's move against the Buddhists apparently emboldened dissident South Vietnamese military leaders, who tried to find out what the Kennedy Administration would do if they attempted to overthrow the Diem regime. U.S. Amb.-to-South Vietnam Henry Cabot Lodge was approached by 2 high-ranking South Vietnamese generals, who denied complicity in the raids and who seemed to want to know how Washington would react to a military coup. Lodge cabled Washington for instructions.

A reply was drafted Aug. 24 by White House aide Michael Forrestal, State Undersecy. Averell Harriman and Roger Hilsman Jr., the State Department's director of Far Eastern affairs. The cable told Lodge to inform the South Vietnamese generals that the U.S. would find it difficult to support South Vietnam with the Nhus in power and unless steps were taken to appease the Buddhists. The generals were to be advised that the U.S. was prepared to support an interim, anti-Communist military government but that a decision to overthrow the Diem government was the prerogative of the South Vietnamese. The cable was sent after being approved by Pres. Kennedy, who was spending the weekend on Cape Cod. Kennedy, however, did not realize that the cable had not been cleared by all of his top advisers, several of whom were away for the weekend.

Kennedy returned to Washington Monday for a meeting of the National Security Council and found, in his words, that the Administration had "fallen apart." Defense Secy. McNamara, Gen. Maxwell D. Taylor, chairman of the Joint Chiefs of Staff, and CIA Director John McCone voiced misgivings about the cable. The President was angered by the division among his advisers and upset because he felt that he had been pushed into approving the cable. He cautioned against undue haste and began retreating from the decision represented by the cable. Additional meetings were held throughout the week as Kennedy sought to obtain agreement among his advisers. By the end of the week, however, it was apparent that the South Vietnamese generals were not prepared to launch a coup at that time. "Perhaps they're afraid to die, like anyone else," observed Lodge.

JFK Explains Attitude Towards Diem & Vietnam

The President's indecision was complicated, moreover, by 2 TV interviews scheduled for Sept. 2 and Sept. 9. On those dates the 2 major TV networks were inaugurating half-hour early evening news programs, and Kennedy had promised to get each off to a good start with an interview. During these broadcasts he was certain to be asked his attitude towards Pres. Diem.

In the CBS interview, conducted by Walter Cronkite at Hyannis Port, Mass., and aired Sept. 2, Kennedy was asked to comment on the current "difficulties" in South Vietnam. "I don't think that unless a greater effort is made by the [Saigon] government to win popular support that the war can be won out there," he said. "In the final analysis, it is their war. They are the ones who have to win it or lose it. We can help them, we can give them equipment, we can send our men out there as advisers, but they have to win it—the people of Vietnam—against the Communists. We are prepared to continue to assist them, but I don't think that the war can be won unless the people support the effort, and, in my opinion, in the last 2 months the government has gotten out of touch with the people. The repressions against the Buddhists, we felt, were very unwise. Now all we can do is to make it very clear that we don't think that this is the way to win. It is my hope that this will become increasingly obvious to the government, that they will take steps to try to bring back popular support for this very essential struggle."

Asked whether he thought the Diem government "still has time to regain the support of the people," Kennedy replied: "I do. With changes in policy and perhaps with personnel, I think it can. If it doesn't make those changes, I would think that the chances of winning it would not be very good."

Kennedy was asked whether it was not obvious that Diem was not about to change his "pattern." He replied: "If he does not change it, of course, that is his decision. He has been there 10 years, and, as I say, he has carried this burden when he has been counted out on a number of occasions. Our best judgment is that he can't be successful on this basis. We hope that he comes to see that, but, in the final analysis, it is the people and the government itself who have to win or lose this struggle. All we can do is help, and we are making it very clear, but I don't agree with those who say we should withdraw. That would be a great mistake. I know people don't like Americans to be engaged in this kind of an effort. 47 Americans have been killed in combat with the enemy, but this is a very important struggle even though it is far away. We took all this—made this effort to defend Europe. Now Europe is quite secure. We also have to participate—[although we] may not like it—in the defense of Asia."

Kennedy thus was thought to be saying that although the war could be won only by the South Vietnamese, the U.S., nevertheless, would not lose heart and withdraw from South Vietnam. He equated the struggle in Vietnam with the post-World War II effort to defend Europe and said that the U.S. had to participate in the defense of Asia.

French Pres. Charles de Gaulle had proposed Aug. 29 that North and South Vietnam be transformed with France's help from a divided, warring country into a unified, neutral state that could assume a new role in Asia. De Gaulle offered French aid and cooperation if North and South Vietnam were prepared to accept such a policy and throw off the foreign "influence" currently wielded by the U.S. and Communist nations. Asked to comment on De Gaulle's proposal, Kennedy, in the Sept. 2 interview, dismissed the suggestion. He noted that since France had no "forces there or any program of economic assistance..., the burden is carried, as it usually is, by the United States and the people there." Kennedy claimed that some Americans were "impatient" with such viewpoints and that "after carrying this load for 18 years, we are glad to get a little counsel, but we would like a little more assistance."

U.S. Probes Problem of Diem

The question of what to do about Diem was discussed again at a Sept. 6 National Security Council meeting. Atty. Gen. Robert Kennedy noted that the U.S. was in South Vietnam to help the people there resist a Communist takeover. The first question, he said, was whether any South Vietnamese regime could defeat the Communists with U.S. help. If it could not, he continued, the thing to do was for the U.S. to quit Vietnam entirely. If, on the other hand, Robert Kennedy concluded, it was possible for a South Vietnamese government, other than the Diem government as currently constituted, to defeat the

Communists, the U.S. owed it to the people of South Vietnam to exert sufficient pressure to bring about the necessary changes. Kennedy added, however, that he did not think that the Administration had the facts to enable it to determine whether or not South Vietnam could be denied to the Communists.

Consequently, it was decided to send Marine Corps Gen. Victor Krulack and Joseph A. Mendenhall of the State Department on a fact-finding mission to South Vietnam. Krulack and Mendenhall left that day, completed their mission in short order, returned Sept. 10, and reported to the National Security Council. Krulack's report was optimistic. He insisted that the war could be won, and he claimed that the war effort had not been unduly affected by the performance of the Diem government. Mendenhall argued that the situation was critical, that the government was on the verge of collapse and that the war could not be won with Diem. After both men had given their reports, Pres. Kennedy asked, "Were you 2 gentlemen in the same country?"

JFK on Diem & the 'Domino Theory'

The subject of Diem and the ("domino theory") came up Sept. 9 when Pres. Kennedy was interviewed on NBC by David Brinkley and Chet Huntley. The President was asked whether the U.S. was prepared to reduce its aid to South Vietnam as a means of forcing the Diem government to undertake reforms. He replied: "I don't think we think that would be helpful at this time. If you reduce your aid, it is possible you could have some effect upon the government structure there. On the other hand, you might have a situation which could bring about a collapse. Strongly in our mind is what happened in the case of China at the end of World War II, where China was lost, a weak government became increasingly unable to control events. We don't want that."

Kennedy was then asked whether he had any reason to doubt the "domino theory," that if South Vietnam fell, the rest of Southeast Asia would follow. He answered: "No, I believe it. I believe it. I think that the struggle is close enough. China is so large, looms so high just beyond the frontiers, that if South Vietnam went, it would not only give them an improved geographic position for a guerrilla assault on Malaya, but would also give the impression that the wave of the future in Southeast Asia was China and the Communists. So I believe it."

Later in the program Kennedy declared: "What I am concerned about is that Americans will get impatient and say, because they don't like events in Southeast Asia or they don't like the government in Saigon, that we should withdraw. That only makes it easy for the Communists. I think we should stay. We should use our influence in as effective way as we can, but we should not withdraw."

(Mrs. Ngo Dinh Nhu assailed Kennedy Sept. 11 as an "appeaser." Arriving in Belgrade to attend a meeting of the Interparliamentary Union, Mrs. Nhu said: "... Pres. Kennedy is a politician, and when he hears a loud opinion speaking in a certain way, he always tries to appease it somehow ... if that opinion is misinformed, the solution is not to bow to it, but the solution should be to inform.")

Kennedy Cools Toward Diem

A further hardening of Pres. Kennedy's attitude towards Pres. Diem seemed evident at the President's press conference Sept. 12. Kennedy apparently sought to dissociate the U.S. from some of Diem's policies. A close reading of his remarks suggested to some observers that he was prepared to accept the replacement of the Diem regime.

"What helps to win the war, we support; what interferes with the war effort, we oppose," Kennedy said. "I have already made it clear that any action by either government which may handicap the winning of the war is inconsistent with our policy or our objectives. This is the test which I think every agency and official of the U.S. government must apply to all our actions, and we shall be applying that test in various ways in the coming months, although I do not think it desirable to state all of our views at this time. I think they will be made more clear as time goes on. But we have a very simple policy in that area, I think. In some ways I think the Vietnamese people and ourselves agree: we want the war to be won, the Communists to be contained, and the Americans to go home. That is our policy. I am sure it is the policy of the people of Vietnam. But we are not there to see a war lost, and we will follow the policy which I have indicated today of advancing those causes and issues which help win the war."

Later in the press conference Kennedy was told that critics of his Vietnam policy were accusing him of acting on the basis of incorrect and inadequate information. Kennedy replied that he was "operating on the basis of, really, the unanimous views and opinions expressed by the most experienced Americans there—in the military, diplomatic, AID agency, the Voice of America and others."

Earlier Sept. 12 Sen. Frank Church (D., Ida.) had introduced in the Senate a resolution calling for an end to U.S. aid to South Vietnam and for the withdrawal of American troops if the government there continued its "cruel repressions." Asked to comment on the resolution, Kennedy said that he thought that "we should stay there and continue to assist South Vietnam" but "that the assistance we give should be used in the most effective way possible."

The Young Democrats of California Sept. 8 adopted a 21-page policy statement calling for the recognition of Communist China and East Germany by the U.S. and the withdrawal of American troops from South Vietnam. Asked about those views, Kennedy said at his Sept. 12 press conference that he didn't "agree with any of them." "I don't know what is happening with the Young Democrats and Young Republicans, but time is on our side," he said.

McNamara & Taylor Probe Situation in Vietnam

Defense Secy. Robert S. McNamara and Gen. Maxwell D. Taylor, chairman of the Joint Chiefs of Staff, visited South Vietnam Sept. 24-Oct. 1 to determine whether the military situation had suffered as a result of the clash between the government and the Buddhists and whether the U.S. should pressure the Diem government to modify its policies. Both officials had previously opposed the so-called "pressure and persuasion" policy on the ground that the political crisis in Vietnam had had little or no effect on the war effort.

McNamara and Taylor returned to Washington Oct. 2 and reported to the President and the National Security Council. The trip had convinced both Taylor and McNamara that a continuation of Diem's repressive policies would be disastrous. Both were currently prepared to exert pressure on Diem, despite the opposition of the American military, which viewed Vietnam as a military rather than a political problem.

In what some authors characterized as a sop to the military and as an effort to keep Pentagon officials from publicly breaking with Kennedy on Vietnam, the White House, following the National Security Council meeting, released a statement confirming the Pentagon's optimistic view of the military situation in Vietnam. The release, prepared by McNamara, stated that "the military program in South Vietnam has made progress" and that "Secy. McNamara and Gen. Taylor reported their judgment that the major part of the U.S. military task can be completed by the end of 1965, although there may be a continuing requirement for a limited number of U.S. training personnel. They reported that by the end of this year [1963] the U.S. program for training Vietnamese should have progressed to the point where 1,000 U.S. military personnel ... can be withdrawn." The statement noted that "the political situation in South Vietnam remains deeply serious. The U.S. has made clear its continuing opposition to any repressive actions in South Vietnam. While such actions have not significantly affected the military effort, they can do so in the future."

In view of the steadily worsening military situation in South Vietnam, many U.S. reporters and civilian officials there described the White House statement as mere political rhetoric. It was felt by many that the true significance of the Taylor-McNamara mission was that the Kennedy Administration no longer believed that the war was being won and was no longer committed to the so-called "sink or swim with Ngo Dinh Diem" policy.

U.S. Cuts Aid to Diem

No formal announcement was made concerning a Kennedy Administration decision to apply pressure on Diem. The *N.Y. Times* reported Oct. 7 that the U.S. had suspended commercial export assistance to South Vietnam. Under the program, imports, mostly from the U.S., were purchased with dollars and bought by Vietnamese merchants with local currency. The U.S. was reported Oct. 21 to have taken these 2 additional economic reprisals against the Diem regime: (1) The U.S. had warned that it would deny funds to the Special Forces if its troops were used for political and security missions instead of fighting the Viet Cong. (2) The U.S. refused to renew its annual agreement to send $4 million worth of condensed milk to South Vietnam; this item had been selected for suspension because Mrs. Ngo Dinh Nhu had been quoted as saying the South Vietnamese did not like condensed milk and had therefore been feeding it to hogs.

The CIA (Central Intelligence Agency) chief of operations in South Vietnam, John H. Richardson, flew back to Washington Oct. 5 after having been recalled for consultations by Pres. Kennedy amid reports that Amb. Lodge was seeking his replacement because of a dispute over the military and political situation in Vietnam. According to various reports, Lodge had complained that his position as head of the U.S. mission in Vietnam conflicted with that of Richardson, who did not confine his operations to gathering and analyzing intelligence information but who worked closely on operational matters with Ngo Dinh Nhu; Lodge and many State Department officials favored a tougher attitude than the CIA toward the South Vietnamese government in its conduct of the U.S.-supported war.

By its actions, many observers said later, the U.S. was in effect encouraging a *coup d'etat* by letting it be known that U.S. support formerly directed towards the Diem regime was currently aimed exclusively at the war against the Communists.

(At about this time Pres. Kennedy made an unsuccessful attempt to get a publisher to remove a critical reporter from Vietnam. Arthur Ochs Sulzberger, newly appointed publisher of the *N.Y. Times,* paid a courtesy call on Kennedy at the White House Oct. 22. Virtually at the beginning of their conversation, Kennedy asked Sulzberger if he did not think that the *Times* reporter in Vietnam, David Halberstam, 29, had become too "involved" with the situation and whether the *Times* was planning to transfer Halberstam to another area. Sulzberger responded negatively, and the *Times* immediately canceled Halberstam's scheduled 2-week vacation lest it appear to have succumbed to Presidential pressure. Halberstam, who had been reporting since July 1962 on what he saw as a steadily worsening situation in South Vietnam, had become an irritant to Kennedy. Since the *Times* was the only newspaper with a full-time correspondent in

Vietnam, Halberstam's coverage was particularly influential. At one point Kennedy was reported to have exclaimed: "I'll be damned if I intend to let my foreign policy be run by a 27-year-old reporter." In 1964 Halberstam won a Pulitzer Prize for his coverage of the Vietnamese war.)

Diem Deposed & Slain in Military Coup

Discontented South Vietnamese army officers overthrew the government in a violent *coup d'etat* Nov. 1-2. They ousted Ngo Dinh Diem as president, killed Diem and his brother, Ngo Dinh Nhu, and installed a civil-military government. Reforms were pledged to revitalize the nation in its war against the Viet Cong. In his book *A Thousand Days,* Arthur Schlesinger Jr. reported seeing Kennedy soon after he learned of Diem's death. According to Schlesinger, the President was somber and shaken. "I had not seen him so depressed since the Bay of Pigs," Schlesinger said. "No doubt he realized that Vietnam was his greatest failure in foreign policy, and that he had never really given it his full attention. But the fact that the Vietnamese seemed ready to fight made him feel that there was a reasonable chance of making a go of it."

In an interview published in the *N.Y. Times* June 30, 1964 Lodge said: "The U.S. was not involved in the overthrow of the Diem regime. The U.S. was trying to change—bring about a change in the behavior of the Diem regime. It was trying to bring about a change in the personnel of the Diem regime.... We were trying to bring about this by thoroughly legitimate political means.... The overthrow was—of the Diem regime—was a purely Vietnamese affair. We never participated in the planning. We never gave any advice. We had nothing whatever to do with it. I—there were opportunities to participate in the planning and to give advice, and we never did. We were punctilious in drawing that line."

According to John Mecklin, U.S. public affairs officer in Vietnam 1962-4, "this was surely an admission that the coup was not a surprise to Lodge. It also implied that he knew something about who was planning it." In his book *Mission in Torment,* Mecklin said that "to assert that the U.S. was not 'involved' in the coup was a bit like claiming innocence for a night watchman at a bank who tells a known safecracker that he is going out for a beer."

The U.S. recognized the provisional government Nov. 7, one day after the new regime had requested recognition. State Secy. Rusk predicted Nov. 8 that the anti-Diem coup would give the South Vietnamese the "impetus" to combat the Viet Cong guerrillas. Rusk said the U.S. hoped the new regime "will be able to rally the country ... so that [it] can be independent and free and secure." The resumption of the U.S.' commodity-import program for South Vietnam was announced by Washington officials Nov. 9.

Asked to comment at his Nov. 14 press conference on the South Vietnamese coup, Kennedy said he hoped it would mean an "increased effort in the war." The purpose of a planned Nov. 20 Honolulu meeting for top Administration and military officials, he said, was "to attempt to assess the situation: what American policy should be, and what our aid policy should be, how we can intensify the struggle, how we can bring Americans out of there." His Administration's object, he went on, "is to bring Americans home, permit the South Vietnamese to maintain themselves as a free and independent country, and permit democratic forces within the country to operate—which they can, of course, much more freely when the assault from the inside, and which is manipulated from the north, is ended."

Day of Pres. Kennedy's Assassination

Pres. Kennedy began a 2-day tour of Texas Nov. 21. Addressing the Fort Worth Chamber of Commerce at breakfast Nov. 22, Kennedy said: His Administration had "increased our special counter-insurgency forces whioh are now engaged in Vietnam by 600%. I hope those who want a stronger America and place it on some signs will also place those figures next to it."

After the breakfast at the Texas Hotel in Fort Worth, Kennedy flew to Love Field, Dallas. There he acknowledged greetings for a brief period and then entered an open car. The motorcade traveled along a 10-mile route through downtown Dallas on its way to the Trade Mart, where the President planned to speak at a luncheon. At approximately 12:30 p.m. CST he was struck by 2 bullets fired by Lee Harvey Oswald. Kennedy was pronounced dead at 1 p.m., Nov. 22, 1963.

Lyndon B. Johnson became President when John F. Kennedy died. Johnson pledged Nov. 24 that his Administration would continue to pursue the U.S. policies on South Vietnam that had been established by Kennedy.

According to British journalist Louis Heren (in *No Hail, No Farewell*), John F. Kennedy left "to his successor a terrible mess the like of which few Presidents had inherited since the other Johnson succeeded the murdered Lincoln." The Washington journalist I. F. Stone wrote in his *Weekly* a short while after Kennedy's death: "He died in time to be remembered as he would like to be remembered, as ever young, still victorious, struck down undefeated, with almost all the potentates and rulers of mankind, friend and foe, come to mourn at the bier. For somehow one has the feeling that in the tangled dramaturgy of events, this sudden assassination was for the author the only satisfactory way out. The Kennedy Administration was approaching an impasse, certainly at home, quite possibly abroad, from which there seemed no escape."

After Kennedy's death many commentators and former associates of the late President speculated at length about what Kennedy would have done about Vietnam had he lived to complete his term and to be reelected in 1964. One of the most significant comments to date has come from Kenneth O'Donnell, Kennedy's appointments secretary at the White House. In an Aug. 7, 1970 article in *Life* magazine, excerpted from a forthcoming book, O'Donnell asserted that Kennedy had decided by 1963 to withdraw all U.S. troops from South Vietnam by the end of 1965, although he planned to delay such an announcement until after the 1964 election.

According to O'Donnell, Pres. Kennedy first began to have doubts about Vietnam in 1961 when both Gen. Douglas MacArthur and Gen. Charles de Gaulle warned against fighting a non-nuclear war on the Asian mainland. During the course of a 3-hour meeting with Kennedy in 1961, MacArthur was said to have called the "domino theory" ridiculous in a nuclear age and to have told Kennedy that the nation's domestic problems were more important than Vietnam. According to O'Donnell, "Kennedy came out of the meeting stunned. That a man like MacArthur should give him such unmilitary advice impressed him enormously."

Late in 1962, following a trip to Vietnam, Sen. Mike Mansfield, according to O'Donnell, advised Kennedy to withdraw U.S. forces from South Vietnam, "a suggestion that startled the President." After his meeting with Mansfield, O'Donnell reported, Kennedy said: "I got angry with Mike for disagreeing with our policy so completely, and I got angry with myself because I found myself agreeing with him."

In the spring of 1963, according to O'Donnell's account, Mansfield, at a White House breakfast for Congressional leaders, criticized the U.S.' Vietnam policies. After the meeting, Kennedy invited Mansfield to his office. O'Donnell, who was present for part of that meeting, reported that Kennedy told Mansfield that he then agreed with him on the need for a complete military withdrawal from Vietnam. Kennedy, however, said, according to O'Donnell, that "I can't do it until 1965—after I'm reelected." After Mansfield left, O'Donnell reported, Kennedy told him (O'Donnell): "In 1965, I'll be damned everywhere as a Communist appeaser. But I don't care. If I tried to pull out completely now, we would have another Joe McCarthy Red scare on our hands, but I can do it after I'm reelected. So we had better make damned sure that I *am* reelected."

Asked on a later occasion (by O'Donnell) how the U.S. could withdraw from Vietnam without losing prestige, Kennedy was quoted by O'Donnell as saying: "Easy. Put a government in there that will ask us to leave."

Following the release of O'Donnell's article Sen. Mansfield was reported by the *Washington Post* Aug. 3, 1970 to have confirmed O'Donnell's account concerning the withdrawal of U.S. forces from Vietnam. "He had definitely and unequivocally made that decision," Mansfield was quoted as saying. Commenting on his 1963 meeting with Kennedy following the Congressional breakfast, Mansfield was further quoted as saying: "Pres. Kennedy didn't waste words. He was pretty sparse with his language. But it was not unusual for him to shift position. There is no doubt that he had shifted definitely and unequivocally on Vietnam, but he never had the chance to put the plan [the 1965 withdrawal] into effect."

In an interview published in the *Washington Post* Aug. 4 O'Donnell said that he did not think Kennedy had told State Secy. Dean Rusk about his plans for withdrawal but that he believed that Defense Secy. Robert S. McNamara had been informed. According to O'Donnell, the idea was never presented in clear terms to the National Security Council (whose sessions O'Donnell had attended.) Robert Kennedy knew of the plan, O'Donnell was reported to have said, but he refused to discuss it during his 1968 political campaign for fear of appearing "cheesey."

O'Donnell's *Life* article appeared in the midst of his unsuccessful campaign for the Democratic nomination for governor of Massachusetts.

In discussing O'Donnell's article, Tom Wicker, a close student of the Kennedy Presidency, noted in his Aug. 4, 1970 column in the *N.Y. Times* that "others who believe themselves knowledgeable about Mr. Kennedy differ" with O'Donnell. "It often has been pointed out," Wicker wrote, "that Mr. Johnson ordered military intervention in 1965 while surrounded by virtually the same advisers who would have counseled Mr. Kennedy, had he lived. Moreover, it was Mr. Kennedy, not Mr. Johnson, who ordered the first substantial 'escalation' in late 1961." According to Wicker, Kennedy's last major statements on the war "are conflicting."

The most significant factor, according to Wicker, "however, probably is not what Mr. Kennedy said, but what he had experienced. By late 1963, it must be remembered, he had suffered in the Bay of Pigs episode both a defeat and a disillusioning exposure to military solutions; he had tested himself against the redoubtable Khrushchev; in the 1962 missile crisis, he made plain to the world his personal strength and determination. None of that proves that he would have refused to intervene in Vietnam. It does suggest that he would not have been under quite the same human and political pressures as those that undoubtedly acted on Mr. Johnson in 1965 and on Richard M. Nixon in Apr. 1970" (when he sent U.S. troops into Cambodia).

ROBERT FRANCIS KENNEDY

Robert F. Kennedy

ROBERT KENNEDY AS HAWK: 1962-5

Robert F. Kennedy—"Bobby" to both friend and foe—served under his brother and his brother's successor as U.S. Attorney General from 1961 to 1964. The New York State Democratic Party nominated him for the U.S. Senate Sept. 1, 1964. Successful in his campaign against the Republican incumbent, Kenneth Keating, Kennedy served in the Senate until his assassination in June 1968. An early supporter and architect of the U.S. military intervention in Vietnam, he later became one of its sharpest critics.

Robert Kennedy shared Pres. Kennedy's interest in guerrilla warfare and counter-insurgency. Like John Kennedy, Robert Kennedy believed that the security of the U.S. was dependent on its ability to prevent and to defeat Communist-led insurrections. Following the abortive Bay of Pigs landing in Cuba in 1961, Pres. Kennedy appointed Robert Kennedy to a high-level committee to review the episode. After the committee completed its work, Robert Kennedy was one of a small group of high-ranking officials appointed to supervise U.S. counter-insurgency efforts. In 1961 and 1962 counter-insurgency was one of Robert Kennedy's major interests. He read and quoted Mao Tse-tung and Che Guevara and was deeply influenced by the writings of Sir Robert Thompson, the man commonly credited with the defeat of the Communist-led insurrection in Malaya in the late 1940s-early 1950s. Within the government, Robert Kennedy was viewed as "Mr. Counter-Insurgency."

RFK Backs U.S. Action in Vietnam

Robert Kennedy toured the Far East in Feb. 1962, 3 months after Pres. Kennedy's decision to increase the U.S. involvement in Vietnam. The visit to the Far East was part of a 30,000-mile trip around the world. At a press conference Feb. 10 in Hong Kong he stated bluntly: "The solution there [in Vietnam] lies in our winning it. This is what the President intends to do."

At a news conference Feb. 18 during a brief stop in Saigon, Kennedy expounded his views on the war: "This is a new kind of war, but war it is in a very real sense of the word. It is a war fought not by massive divisions but secretly by terror, assassinations, ambush and infiltration. Hanoi may deny its responsibility but the guilt is clear. In a flagrant violation of its signed pledge at Geneva in 1954, the North Vietnamese regime has launched on a course to destroy the Republic of Vietnam."

A British newsman asked: "American boys are dying out here. Do the American people understand and approve what is going on?" Kennedy replied: "I think the American people understand and fully support this struggle. Americans have great affection for the people of Vietnam. I think the United States will do what is necessary to help a country that is trying to repel aggression with its own blood, tears, and sweat."

Robert Kennedy wrote a book, *Just Friends and Brave Enemies,* in which he reviewed his world trip and said: "We must meet our duty and convince the world that we are." He reported that when he reached Saigon, "Pres. Diem's brother came out to meet the plane, and a number of our own officials, military and civilian, also came out to the airport. Far from home, they fully realized the possibility that Southeast Asia might explode in the near future. It was clear that they wondered if the people in the United States knew. In a brief statement to the press about the struggle under way in Vietnam, I ... [said] that the President [John F. Kennedy] 'has been extremely impressed with the courage and determination of the people of your country and he has pledged the United States to stand by the side of Vietnam through this very difficult and troublesome time. We will win in Vietnam, and we shall remain here until we do.' "

Back home Robert Kennedy sought to justify the increased U.S. involvement in the war and reiterated the Administration's intention to remain in Vietnam until the war was won. He said at the national commander's dinner of the American Legion Convention in Las Vegas, Nev. Oct. 9, 1962:

"I am sure you understand more than most the conditions under which several thousand of our fellow Americans are serving in the undeclared war in South Vietnam. They are there because last November a comprehensive program was initiated calling for many forms of American aid to reverse the trend in South Vietnam. This included military assistance to the friendly forces combatting the Communists, economic assistance to the villagers who were the Communists' principal target and administrative and technical assistance to bolster the Vietnam government....

"The courageous effort under way in South Vietnam is not the only governmental response to the threat of guerrilla warfare. In Washington, a special group of senior officials—reporting directly to the President—supervises the development and use of all defense assets which can play a role in counter-insurgency. One example of the activities of this special group has been to overhaul the instruction in the Departments of State and Defense, as well as in all other agencies which participate in counter-insurgency programs. Between now and next June some 57,000 government officials, many having high rank and vast experience, will attend courses dealing with counter-insurgency.

"Last June at West Point, Pres. Kennedy described this new challenge to the graduating class in these words: 'This is another type of war, new in its intensity, ancient in its origin—war by guerrillas, subversives, insurgents, assassins, war by ambush instead of combat; by infiltration instead of aggression, seeking victory by eroding and exhausting the enemy instead of engaging him. It is a form of warfare uniquely adapted to what has been strangely called "wars of liberation," to undermine the efforts of new and poor countries to maintain the freedom that they have finally achieved. It preys on economic unrest and ethnic conflicts. It requires in those situations where we must counter it ... if freedom is to be saved, a whole new kind of strategy, a wholly different kind of force, and therefore a new and wholly different kind of military training.'

"Many of you know what is involved in this effort. In Malaya, the Communist guerrilla war lasted from 1946 to 1957. It involved 400,000 armed men and caused nearly 16,000 casualties. In Greece the period of conflict was from 1945 to 1950. 300,000 men were involved, and 130,000 casualties were inflicted. You know that this kind of warfare can be long, drawn out and costly, but if communism is to be stopped, it is necessary. And we mean to see this job through to the finish."

U.S. Build-Up Against Guerrillas

Like Pres. Kennedy and key military and civilian officials, Robert Kennedy said that the infusion of American aid and advisers into South Vietnam had robbed the enemy of its initiative. "We have taken major steps in recent months to strengthen the frontiers of freedom," Kennedy said in a speech at the Seattle World's Fair Aug. 7, 1962. "The proof of our progress is that the reservists who were called up last summer at a time of crisis are now returning to their homes all across the country. Where a year ago the situation in South Vietnam was dark, the forces of national independence now have a fighting chance."

Speaking at the North Carolina Cold War Seminar in Asheville, May 17, 1963, Robert Kennedy said that the U.S. "must be ready to meet war by guerrillas, subversives, insurgents, assassins, war by ambush instead of combat." Now "for the first time, we have that capability," he claimed; the Kennedy Administration had done the following "to deal with Communist guerrilla attacks and Communist-inspired insurgency": "(1) A special committee of high officials in Washington now supervises our counter-insurgency efforts on a continuing basis; (2) by next month, some 57,000 government officials will have completed counter-insurgency courses; (3) the Army Special Warfare Forces are now 6 times stronger than in 1961; and (4) special training is now carried out in several languages at the Special Warfare Center here in your own state at Ft. Bragg, the Police Academy and Jungle Warfare Training Center in Panama and at training centers in Europe, Okinawa and Vietnam." "That these are only steps in a long and hard struggle is evident," Kennedy conceded. "But I believe the tide has turned. I believe it is within our ability to keep world communism on the defensive, and we intend to do just that."

Kennedy said in a speech at the California Institute of Technology June 8, 1964:

"We are agreed that American nuclear superiority is essential to unanimous nuclear restraint. But as we all know so well, the actual fighting since World War II has not involved nuclear weapons or even conventional warfare. It was in 1937 that Mao Tse-tung wrote: 'The guerrilla campaigns being waged in China today are a page in history that has no precedent. Their influence will be confined not solely to China in her present anti-Japanese struggle, but will be worldwide.' That prophecy has proved accurate. We have seen it in Malaya and Greece, the Philippines and Cuba. We have seen the streets of Caracas become the front line of this era, and Communist guerrillas are fighting today over all of South Vietnam and Laos and at the outskirts of Bukavu in the Congo. The struggle has been broadened today to include violence and terrorist activities that could not even be described as guerrilla warfare. And this really has vastly increased the importance of local police forces and those who preserve an internal defense....

"We have made a beginning. We have achieved some notable successes, but we have not mastered the art. More importantly, perhaps, in a practical sense, we have not perfected the technique of training foreign nationals to defend themselves against Communist terrorism and guerrilla penetration. Having an adequate defense against terrorism is only part of the answer, however. To the extent that guerrilla warfare and terrorism arise from the conditions of a desperate people, we know that they cannot be put down by force alone. The people themselves must have some hope for the future. There must be a realistic basis for faith in some alternative to communism. It is for that reason that the United States must continue to expand its efforts to reach the peoples of other nations—particularly young people in the rapidly developing southern continents. Governments may come and go, but in the long run, the future will be determined by the needs and aspirations of these young people. Over the years, an understanding of what America really stands for is going to count far more than missiles, aircraft carriers and supersonic bombers. The big changes of the future will result from this understanding—or lack of it.

"We have made some progress in reaching the peoples of other countries. The aid and information programs, the Peace Corps, Presidential trips abroad, are all ways of getting beyond mere government-to-government contact. But the critical moves—the moves that will determine our success—are the kinds of political choices this country makes in picking its friends abroad—and its enemies. Far too often, for narrow tactical reasons, this country has associated itself with tyrannical and unpopular regimes that had no following and no future. Over the past 20 years we have paid dearly because of support given to colonial rulers, cruel dictators or ruling cliques void of social purpose. This was one of Pres. Kennedy's gravest concerns. It would be one of his proudest achievements if history records his administration as an era of political friendships made for the United States. He valued most highly the cooperation established with the India of Nehru, the rallying of democratic leaders in Latin America to the Alliance for Progress, the support won from all the new African states for the American position on the Congo.

"It is these examples and others like them now being advanced by Pres. Johnson which will go a long way to determine our future. By achieving harmony with broadly based governments concerned with their own peoples, we do more than make our way easier for a year or 2. We create for this country the opening to the future that is so essential. Ultimately, communism must be defeated by progressive political programs which wipe out the poverty, misery and discontent on which it thrives. For that reason, progressive political programs are the best way to erode the Communist presence in Latin America, to turn back the Communist thrust into Southeast Asia and to insure the stability of the new African nations and preserve stability in the world...."

In June 1964, 7 months after Pres. Kennedy's death, Robert Kennedy sent a brief note to Pres. Johnson offering to serve in South Vietnam "in any capacity" should U.S. Amb. Henry Cabot Lodge resign. But Johnson urged Kennedy to stay on as Attorney General, especially in view of anticipated civil rights problems. (Lodge resigned June 23 to help Gov. William Scranton of Pennsylvania in his campaign for the Republican nomination for President. Lodge was replaced in Saigon by Gen. Maxwell Taylor, chairman of the Joint Chiefs of Staff.)

RFK Elected to Senate

In 1964, the year he resigned from the cabinet and was elected to the Senate, Robert Kennedy wrote another book, *Pursuit of Justice.* In a chapter on counter-insurgency he reviewed U.S. efforts to date in South Vietnam. "This kind of warfare can be long-drawn-out and costly," he said, "but if communism is to be stopped, it is necessary. And we mean to see this job through to the finish.... Out in the field the dreadful battle against the guerrilla continues. Several thousand of our fellow Americans are serving in the undeclared war in South Vietnam. They are there because of a comprehensive program calling for many forms of American aid to reverse the trend in South Vietnam. This includes military assistance to the friendly forces combating the Communists, economic assistance to the villagers who were the Communists' principal target, and administrative and technical assitance to bolster the Vietnam government."

Vietnam was not an issue in Kennedy's 1964 Senate campaign. His most comprehensive, if somewhat muddled, statement on the war was given in a radio station WINS interview Oct. 25, 1964, 2 weeks before the election. Asked what advice he would give the President about Vietnam if he were elected to the Senate, Kennedy replied: "... Basically, the problem is that there has to be the support of the people for the military effort that is being made, has to be support of the people for the government. We've had overturn of the government on 3 different occasions now, and I think it makes it difficult when the wars have been going on for 25 years so that the country lacks that kind of stability, and there is tremendous exhaustion by the people, and the fact that you have this guerrilla warfare that goes on continuously.... I think that the people have to feel that there is political progress being made and that they can be protected in their communities, protected in their villages, and I think that once there is that confidence, then I think the war will be won."

1965 Policy Debate

The Johnson Administration's Vietnam policy was the subject of sharp domestic debate during 1965. Opposition to the Administration's handling of the Vietnam problem came largely from liberal Democrats who favored limiting or ending the U.S. military intervention and from some Republicans who demanded intensification of the air war against North Vietnam and steps to assure a military defeat of Communist forces in South Vietnam. Despite vociferous objections from both groups, which included respected members of the Senate, an overwhelming majority of Democrats and Republicans continued to support Johnson in pressing the war until Communist forces withdrew from South Vietnam or accepted unconditional peace negotiations.

Democratic and Republican Congressional leaders Feb. 8 voiced strong support of Johnson's decision to order retaliatory air strikes against North Vietnam. Senate majority leader Mike Mansfield (D., Mont.) said: It was the President's aim "to achieve stability if possible so that the Vietnamese government can manage its own affairs within South Vietnam. I think he is proceeding cautiously and carefully, and he has a very full appreciation of all the elements involved in any move he directs." Senate minority leader Everett McK. Dirksen (R., Ill.) said that "if we hadn't given an adequate response, we might have given the impression we might pull out" of South Vietnam. But Sen. Wayne Morse (D., Ore.), calling the attacks "a black page in American history," suggested that "this threat to world peace" be negotiated at an international conference through the UN or the 1954 Geneva accords on Indochina. Sen. Ernest Gruening (D., Alaska) also proposed that the war "be brought to the conference table, the sooner the better."

Opposition to the war was also mounting outside Congress. New York police Feb. 14 arrested 14 persons blocking the entrances of the U.S.' UN mission. The demonstration, against the U.S.' Vietnamese policies, was organized by the Committee for Non-Violent Action. Police Feb. 20 arrested 19 more committee demonstrators led by Rev. A.J. Muste, head of the committee, when they refused to halt picketing at the Hilton Hotel, where a Peace on Earth convocation was in progress. Similar rallies protesting U.S. policy were held near the UN building and in other parts of the city, and more than 400 students picketed the White House.

RFK Supports Administration

In a speech in Ithaca, N.Y. Feb. 23, 1965, Robert Kennedy held that the U.S. should keep its forces in South Vietnam to fulfill a commitment there. But he said he was "not in favor of staying a minute more than is necessary." "The United States has made a commitment to help Vietnam," Kennedy asserted. "I'm in favor of keeping that commitment and taking whatever steps are necessary. If our word means anything, we must remain as long as it is evident evident that the people favor it."

The Senate May 6 debated a supplemental appropriations bill for the U.S. war effort in Vietnam. 3 Senators, Wayne Morse, Ernest Gruening and Gaylord Nelson (D., Wis.), voted against the measure. In his first major Senate speech on the war, Robert Kennedy announced his support of the bill. Withdrawal or enlargement of the war were contrary to the national interest, he said. The best course was to seek an honorable settlement by negotiations, which "I take it is the policy of the Administration," he said. Kennedy told the Senate:

"I vote for this resolution because our fighting forces in Vietnam and elsewhere deserve the unstinting support of the American government and the American people. I do so in the understanding that, as Sen. [John C.] Stennis [D., Miss.] said yesterday: 'It is not a blank check .... We are backing up our men and also backing up the present policy of the President. If he substantially enlarges or changes it, I would assume he would come back to us in one way or another.'

"We confront 3 possible courses in Vietnam:

"The first is the course of withdrawal. Such a course would involve a repudiation of commitments undertaken and confirmed by 3 administrations. It would imply an acquiescence in Communist domination of south Asia—a domination unacceptable to the peoples of the area struggling to control and master their own destiny. It would be an explicit and gross betrayal of those in Vietnam who have been encouraged by our support to oppose the spread of communism. It would promote an inexorable tendency in every capital to rush to Peiping [Peking] and make the best possible bargain for themselves. It would gravely—perhaps irreparably—weaken the democratic position in Asia.

"The 2d is the course of purposely enlarging the war.... This would be a deep and terrible decision. We cannot hope to win a victory over Hanoi by such remote and antiseptic means as sending bombers off aircraft carriers. I have understood the purpose of the raids that have been conducted so far have been to indicate to Peiping and Hanoi our resolve to meet our commitments. I do not believe we should be under the self-delusion that this military effort will bring Ho Chi Minh or the Viet Cong to their knees. The course of enlarging the war would mean the commitment to Vietnam of hundreds of thousands of American troops. It would tie our forces down in a terrain far more difficult than that of Korea, with lines of communication and supply far longer and more vulnerable. It would risk the entry of the Chinese Communists and their inexhaustible reserves of ground troops. It would force the Soviet Union, now engaged in a bitter contest with Peiping for the leadership of the world Communist movement, to give major assistance to Hanoi, and it might well temporarily revive the relations between Peiping and Moscow. It would lead to heavy pressure on our own government by thoughtless people for the use of nuclear weapons, and it might easily lead to nuclear warfare and the 3d world war.

"Both of these courses—withdrawal and enlargement—are contrary to the interests of the United States and to humanity's hope for peace.

"There remains a 3d course—and this, I take it, is the policy of the Administration, the policy we are endorsing today. This is the course of honorable negotiation. This is the hope of ending the violation of the northern frontier of South Vietnam and of moving toward a settlement of conditions in this troubled land—a settlement which would in the end unite South Vietnam, Laos, Cambodia and North Vietnam in a common determination to live at peace with their neighbors, to reduce the intervention and presence of foreign troops and ideologies and to join together in undertakings, like the development of the Mekong River Valley, of benefit to all the people of the whole area.

"Along with a number of Senators, I have taken advantage of Pres. Johnson's cordial invitation to discuss these matters with him. He has listened to my comments on the course of the war in Vietnam, and I have appreciated the courtesy and interest with which he has heard these thoughts. Pres. Johnson has expressed our American desire for honorable negotiations. So far there has been no satisfactory response. It seems that North Vietnam thinks it will win anyway and therefore sees no point in negotiation. To create the atmosphere for negotiation in these conditions, we must show Hanoi that it cannot win the war, and that we are determined to meet our commitments no matter how difficult. This is the reason and the necessity, as I understand it, for the military action of our government.

"But I believe we should continue to make clear to Hanoi, to the world, and to our own people that we are interested in discussions for settlement. I believe that our efforts for peace should continue with the same intensity as our efforts in the military field. I believe that we have erred for some time in regarding Vietnam as purely a military problem when in its essential aspects it is also a political and diplomatic problem. I would wish, for example, that the request for appropriations today had made provision for programs to better the lives of the people of South Vietnam. For success will depend not only on protecting the people from aggression but on giving them the hope of a better life which alone can fortify them for the labor and sacrifice ahead."

The right to dissent against U.S. policy in Vietnam was defended by Robert Kennedy in a speech at the Queens College commencement in New York June 15. Kennedy said: "It is not helpful, it is not honest, to protest the war in Vietnam as if it were a simple and easy question.... But the complexity and difficulty of any situation should not keep you from speech or action." (According to Jack Newfield [in *Robert Kennedy: A Memoir,* published in June 1969], "By making the right to dissent an issue, Kennedy was able to postpone taking a position on the heart of the matter, the bombings of North Vietnam and the disinclination of the American government to negotiate with the Viet Cong. A similar ploy was used by Edward Kennedy during 1967, when he placed the plight of the 2 million Vietnamese refugees at the center of his concerns, rather than the bombing, escalation, negotiations, a coalition government in Saigon, or the undemocratic nature of the South Vietnamese elections.")

In July 1965 Adam Walinsky, one of Sen. Kennedy's young speech writers, wrote a speech for Kennedy to deliver July 9 at the International Police Academy commencement in Washington. Walinsky's draft contained several paragraphs seemingly critical of Administration policy in Vietnam. Kennedy approved the speech at about 3:30 p.m. July 8, the day before it was to be delivered. Copies of the speech were then sent to the news media. Within the hour newsmen phoned Kennedy's office to ask whether he was going to begin an extensive campaign against Administration war policies. That evening Kennedy removed from the speech the paragraphs that seemed to criticize Administration policy. Passages deleted included:

● "If all a government can promise its people in response to insurgent activity, is 10 years of napalm and heavy artillery, it would not be a government for long."

● "Victory in a revolutionary war is won not by escalation but by deescalation."

● "Air attacks by a government on its own villages are likely to be far more dangerous and costly to the people than is the individual and selective terrorism of an insurgent movement."

Kennedy's speech, as delivered, suggested that effective counter-insurgency required political as well as military solutions. The many revolutionary campaigns launched since World War II, including Vietnam, "offer us lessons for the future, for the decades of revolutionary war which are the challenge ahead," he asserted. In the speech Kennedy said:

"Pres. Kennedy said in 1961, technology has made all-out war highly unlikely because if it comes it means the end of civilization as we know it. And we are faced instead, he said, with 'another kind of war—new in its intensity, ancient in its origin—war by guerrillas, subversives, insurgents, assassins, war by ambush instead of by combat; by infiltration, instead of aggression, seeking victory by eroding and exhausting the enemy instead of engaging him.'

"This war has worn many faces. It has been a war for independence from external domination, as in Algeria and Cyprus and Hungary. It has been a war for regional or tribal identity, as in Burma or Iraq or in the Naga Hills of India. And it has been a war for communism, as in Malaya or Venezuela or South Vietnam...."

"At the moment, our most prominent problem is in Vietnam. We must realize, however, that Vietnam has become more and more an open military conflict as well, in which military action on our part is essential just to allow the government to act politically. What I say today is in the hope that the lessons of the last 20 years will be applied in other places—so that we are able to win these wars before they reach the stage of all-out military conflict now apparent in South Vietnam.

"I am a citizen of a nation which itself was born in a war for national liberation. It would be against our deepest traditions to oppose any genuine popular revolution. But acts of aggression, masquerading as national revolutions, pose a difficult problem. Revolutionary wars carried on with the outside support of the Soviet Union, or of China, or of others of their allies, offer the greatest threat to the world order of free and independent states to which all nations pledged themselves in the charter of the United Nations.

"But if these conflicts are called wars, and have deep international consequences, they are at the same time not wars—and their outcome is determined by internal factors. For their essence is political—a struggle for the control of government, a contest for the allegiance of men. Allegiance is won as in any political contest—by an idea and a faith, by promise and performance. Governments resist such challenges only by being effective and responsive to the needs of their people.

"Effective and representative government can, of course, take many forms. What is right for the United States may not be right for your countries, and others would have still other convictions on the precise form government should take—on ownership and control of the means of production, on the distribution of riches and the level of taxation, on the range of domestic and international policy. These questions must always be for each nation and people to decide for itself. So long as their choice is their own, not imposed from outside or by dictatorship of left or right, it must be respected by all others. If we wish to encourage the spread of democracy and freedom, primary reliance must be on the force of our example: on the qualities of the societies we build in our own countries—what we stand for at home and abroad.

"In the 1960s, it should not be necessary to repeat that the great struggle of the coming decades is one for the hearts and minds of men. But too often, of late, we have heard instead the language of gadgets—of force-ratios and oil-blots, techniques and technology—of bombs or grenades which explode with special violence, of guns which shoot around corners, of new uses for helicopters and special vehicles.

"Men's allegiance, however, and this kind of war, are *not* won by superior force, by the might of numbers or by the sophistication of technology. On the tiny island of Cyprus, the British Army had 110 soldiers and policemen for every member of EOKA, which never numbered more than a few hundred terrorists; yet Britain had to surrender control of the island within 5 years after the rebellion began. In the Philippines, by contrast, Ramon Magsaysay had an army of only 50,000 to fight 15,000 Huks who were at the gates of Manila when he took office as defense minister. His forces had no special modern armament; yet within 4 years the Huk rebellion was crushed and its leaders had surrendered.

"But why are mere numbers, or the possession of advanced weapons, not conclusive? And how can these conflicts be won without such force, or modern technology?

"One answer lies in the character of military force itself. Conventional military force—and all our advanced weapons technology—is useful only to destroy. But a government cannot make war on its own people, cannot destroy its own country. To do so is to abandon its reason for existence—its responsibility to its people—and its claim to their allegiance. Suppose, for example, that a government force is fired upon from a village, or that rebels have forced the village to fly the insurgent flag. A government which attacks that village from the air, or with heavy artillery, abandons all pretence of protecting the people of the village—abandons the first duty of any government worthy of the name....

"There is another side to this coin. When an insurgent uprising threatened to unseat Jerome Bonaparte, his brother Napoleon told him, 'Use your bayonets.' Jerome replied, 'Brother, you can do anything with bayonets—except sit on them.' That is still true today.

"Guns and bombs cannot build—cannot fill empty stomachs or educate children, cannot build homes or heal the sick. But these are the ends for which men establish and obey governments; they will give their allegiance only to governments which meet these needs.

"In the Philippines, for example, Magsaysay pursued the Huks vigorously. But he offered much more than conflict to the people. First, he ensured an honest election throughout the country.... 2d, a thorough land reform began; and it was enforced through such devices as special landlord-tenant courts which were held from jeeps so that the judges would be available to peasants in isolated rural areas. There followed many other reforms directed at the welfare of the people.

"We all know the necessity for this political dimension to our actions. Too often, however, it is not given the priority it demands as we allow the military dimension to become more urgent and insistent. But reform, and the hope it brings, cannot be postponed. For insurgents of the modern variety continually institute at least a facsimile of such reforms in every area they control. In Vietnam, in China, in Cuba, to name but 3, Communist insurgents have abolished landlordism, organized adult education classes, established courts and in all areas they occupied—even in many which they controlled only at night. They have thus entered into direct competition with the established government. When the defenders have ignored reform, the hopes of the people could only center on the insurgents. And when a victorious government army is followed by landlords collecting back rents from the peasants, we should not wonder that the insurgents often attract the allegiance of the peasants. It does little good to warn that the end result of communism will be dictatorship and exploitation; the deeds of today speak most loudly—if not most truly—on whose promises will be kept tomorrow.

"A 2d reason for the inadequacy of military action is that it can give no hope. Force is neutral; it has no program. Every insurgent movement lives not primarily on force, but on a dream—of independence, of justice, of progress, of a better life for one's children. For such dreams men will undergo great hardship and sacrifice.... Without a vision of the future to offer, a government can demand no sacrifice, no resistence to insurgent terror or blandishments.

"Not only is the military approach deficient in itself. More dangerously, it tends to obscure and prevent essential political action. In conventional war the aim is to kill the enemy. But the essence of successful counter-insurgency is not to kill but to bring the insurgent back into the national life. In Malaya, the British achieved great success by distributing photographs of prisoners—half-starved and ragged when captured, well-fed and smiling after internment. Bonuses were given for arms turned in to the government, with no questions asked; amnesty was offered to rebels who would surrender. Such devices were carried further in the Philippines; there Huks who surrendered were settled with their families on newly cleared agricultural land of their own. George Marshall once said, 'Let's not talk about this matter too much in military terms; to do so might make it a military problem.' Too often, we forget that wisdom.

"Another central need of counter-insurgency effort is for adherence to fundamental rules of law and fair dealing. It may seem strange to assert that a legal government should bind itself by restrictions, such as the Geneva Convention, in the midst of an assault on its existence. But the government is competing with a rival administration, which often ruthlessly enforces its own rules of fair dealing with the people: no excessive taxation, no stealing (except from the rich), no physical maltreatment (except of those who aid the government). The government must match and overmatch the insurgents in this respect, punishing and rewarding wisely and consistently—as in Malaya, where villages were carefully graded on their help to the rebels, and food and equipment were distributed accordingly....

"Actions such as these are necessary to success. But they are not the kind of measures which follow from thinking of insurgency as conventional war; rather they assume that the insurgents are fellow-citizens who can be and should be returned to the political process. Pres. Kennedy once said that the peace we must seek is 'not the peace of the grave or the security of the slave, [but] genuine peace, the kind of peace that makes life on earth worth living, the kind that enables men and nations to grow and to hope and to build a better life for their children.' That is what we must offer insurgents as well.

"It is sometimes said that political methods are ineffective against terrorists—as in Vietnam, where the Viet Cong have cruelly assassinated over 16,000 local officials. But even the use of terror is limited by political considerations—and can be sharply limited by

political action. Surely it is significant that unprotected Americans of the International
Volunteer Service—who work for the direct benefit of the people—have not been molested
even in the Viet Cong areas, and that of several thousand AID [U.S. Agency for International Development] officials who have served in the countryside there, less than a dozen
have been harmed. Similarly, terrorist action in the last Venezuelan election failed because
public reaction was unfavorable; and it was abandoned.

"It has also been said that an insurgency cannot be put down as long as it is supplied
from, and can seek sanctuary in, a neighboring country. No matter what assistance they
receive from outside, however, insurgents stand or fall on their political success. Without
popular support, they become conventional invaders—and can be dealt with by conventional means.

"I think the history of the last 20 years demonstrates beyond doubt that our approach
to revolutionary war must be political—political first, political last, political always. Where
the needs and grievances of the people begin to be met by the political process, insurgency
loses its popular character and becomes a police problem. . . .

"Military force of varying intensity will undoubtedly be a major component of a
revolutionary war. I would like, in this connection, to make an important distinction. Just
as mere military force cannot win political victories, so military aggression cannot be defeated by solely political means. If guerrillas are infiltrated into a country from outside,
that aggression, like any invasion, must be met by armed force of sufficient power to
defeat it. Where the threat is partly political and partly military, it must be met on both
fronts at once. Each threat is unique—each country is different—and aggression takes
many forms. Each threat must be met on its own grounds, with a response measured to its
scope. To meet the political threat of revolutionary war, then, what are the essential forms
of political action?

"At the outset must be restated the need for effective and responsible government.
Especially is this true in the rural areas in which live from 75% to 90% of the people of the
developing nations. John Mecklin, formerly the Public Affairs Officer in Saigon, has told
of a Vietnamese village which freely gave its allegiance to the Viet Cong. For hundreds of
years, the women of the village had had to circle around a rich man's land to reach the only
village well. The Viet Cong cut a path across this land—and in that simple fashion made a
major change in village life. No money was required—no elaborate equipment—simply a
sensitivity to the village need, and the will to meet that need.

"Most important, we must impart hope—hope for progress, fulfilled as quickly as
circumstances permit. In many countries, land reform is the essential need of the vast
majority of the people; it must receive central priority. Education is always vital—not just
for the cities, not even only for children; but for every peasant who can learn to read, or
drive a tractor, or even use a hoe instead of a forked stick.

"For what we must build, after all, is a nation—a nation in which, as in the Scriptures,
'Your old men shall dream dreams, your young men shall see visions. And where there is no
vision, life shall perish from the earth.'

"We must also build all the other structures that help to make up a stable society—
such as labor unions, and farmer cooperatives for those who work with their hands and
their backs; student groups for the nation's new emerging leaders; political parties to give
all men a voice in the councils of government. The political coloration of these groups is
less important than the fact of their existence; simply by being organized, by being there,
they add stability and permanence. . . .

"Moreover, these groups can be a great force for reform, progress—and action. The
truce in the Bolivian tin miners' strike, for example, was arranged by 2 student leaders.
Major social-action programs in rural Peru are being undertaken by students from the
cities, as are similar programs in India. These student activities are especially important
because as much as 1/2 the population of the nations concerned is under the age of 25, and
the young are often the progressive and dynamic leaders. Magsaysay, Mboya, Nyrere,
Belaunde—and Castro and Nkrumah as well—were leaders of national stature in their 30s.
These young men must have the scope to act within the society—or else they may turn to
action outside the established order.

67

"And then there is your role—the role of the police. Everything I have said thus far—every consideration of political action—depends in large part on you. For if pure military force is not to dominate the scene, you must be the major element in the keeping of order. In your hands will rest the responsibility for security against terrorism. On your shoulders will be the burden of deciding what activity is dangerous agitation and what is healthy reform. For many, perhaps thousands of people, you will represent the government—you will *be* the government. If you do justice, you will build a just and stable order. If you act to improve the lives of your people—with a school house or a small bridge, a road to market or a shorter path to the well—then your government will be effective and responsive....

"In your great task, we must work together. We can help you build a road for defense and administration, as in Northeast Thailand. We can help you dig wells and bring electricity and—as in this course—work with you for improvement of your police capabilities as well. What we cannot do—what only you can do—is bring to your people the leadership and the hope and the understanding they need if your countries are to succeed. Our acts, no matter how intelligent or well-meant, are from the outside. It is your actions that will make a society.

"But one last word of caution: no less than military action, political action in an unjust cause is lost. It is not enough to stand for anti-communism—or for stability—or for order. We all have a responsibility to stand with the people—for justice—for understanding—for progress. If we meet that obligation, we need have no fear for the future, no worry over wars of revolution...."

Again defending "the right to criticize and the right to dissent," Kennedy said Nov. 5, 1965 at a news conference at the University of Southern California: "It would be ironic if dissent from other phases of our country's policy were to damage seriously the programs which dissenters point to as examples of what we should be doing more of." Asked whether he approved of radical student groups sending blood to North Vietnamese victims of American bombings, he replied that he did since it would be "in the oldest tradition of this country." "I am willing to give blood to anybody who needs it," he said. But blood donations to Hanoi should be given only "with concurrence of the government and the supervision of the Red Cross." Kennedy, however, did not contribute any blood himself, nor did he assist or encourage those who did. Barry M. Goldwater condemned Kennedy's remarks as "close to treason."

Nationwide demonstrations against U.S. policy in Vietnam had been held Oct. 15-16 in about 40 U.S. cities. The demonstrations were organized by the National Coordinating Committee to End the War in Vietnam, a student-run organization set up in August with headquarters in Madison, Wis. near the University of Wisconsin campus. In New York, a parade was held Oct. 16, and more than 10,000 demonstrators marched in it despite heckling and threats from counter-demonstrators. In Berkeley, Calif., several thousand students attempted to march Oct. 15 and again Oct. 16 to the Oakland Army Base for a mass "sleep-out"; on both occasions they were turned back at the Oakland city limits by Oakland police. Marchers estimated to number from 15,000 to 35,000 converged on the White House Nov. 27 in a "March on Washington for Peace in Vietnam." The demonstration had been initiated by the National Committee for a Sane Nuclear

Policy (SANE), under the sponsorship of an *ad hoc* committee that included prominent American authors, artists, churchmen and civil rights leaders.

Kennedy reiterated Dec. 5 that he "basically" supported the U.S. position in Vietnam. But he added that he had "some reservations about whether we are doing enough in the economic and political field and...in the diplomatic field." Speaking on the NBC-TV program "Meet the Press," he said that the U.S.' military efforts "cannot by themselves win the war" and that Pres. Johnson should consult Congress before deciding whether to expand further the U.S. military build-up in Vietnam or to widen the air strikes against North Vietnam. Asked whether he favored halting the bombing of North Vietnam as a means of bringing about negotiations, Kennedy answered that he did not. Asked to amplify his statement Kennedy said that he would not favor a unilateral halt in the bombings unless such a move would bring about peace talks.

Late in 1965 Kennedy began to urge that domestic spending programs not be postponed because of the war. He said in a Dec. 16 press release: "Certainly the war in Vietnam will require great sums from the budget; certainly it will impose some strain on our resources; certainly our young men are entitled to all the support we can give them. And all this will require sacrifices on our part as well as theirs. But to limit our action to the support of the war in Vietnam—to postpone action on our pressing domestic needs—would be a terrible mistake. To refuse to make the further efforts and the further sacrifices that justice and tranquility require at home would be to invite the very internal conflagration of which we have been warned—to invite a society so irretrievably split that no war will be worth fighting, and no war will be possible to fight."

Christmas Truce

The National Liberation Front (NLF), political arm of the Viet Cong, proposed Dec. 7 that the 2 sides observe a 12-hour Christmas battlefront truce. A broadcast by the NLF radio said the Viet Cong guerrillas would halt their attacks in South Vietnam from 7 p.m. Christmas Eve until 7 a.m. "to allow people on the other side to celebrate Christmas in peace" provided U.S. and South Vietnamese troops carried no arms. A U.S. State Department response to the NLF bid Dec. 8 said "the real Christmas present for the world would be a readiness to make peace and to accept any of the suggestions made by ourselves and others to move to the conference table." Gen. William C. Westmoreland, commander of U.S. forces in Vietnam, said Dec. 10: "The prospect of fighting is prevalent on any day. Christmas Day is no exception."

Sen. Kennedy suggested Dec. 9 that the U.S. seek an extension of the Viet Cong's 12-hour truce bid. He said such an extension "could be for a certain period of time" or "on an open-end basis," during which time the cease-fire could be continued while certain conditions were complied with, or "certain other arrangements could be made." Peace in Vietnam was urgent, Kennedy said, "because we are getting into a more dangerous situation for all mankind."

Kennedy's Senate office issued a Christmas Eve press release urging that U.S. and South Vietnamese forces not be the first to attack should the Viet Cong choose to extend the battlefield truce. The statement said:

"There are 2 cease-fire periods now established in the Vietnamese conflict. One 12-hour period, announced unilaterally by the Viet Cong, will end at 7:00 a.m. Christmas Day (6:00 p.m. Eastern Standard Time, Dec. 24, 1965). The United States and South Vietnamese governments have themselves ordered a more extended cease-fire period lasting 30 hours and ending at midnight, Christmas Day (11:00 a.m. Eastern Standard Time, Dec. 25, 1965).

"It is my view that American and South Vietnamese troops should not be the first to attack if the Viet Cong substantially honors the additional hours of the truce period established by our side. In this way we should take further advantage of the cease-fire periods themselves in order to provide an avenue by which the conflict can be brought from the battlefield to the conference table. There should also be a restatement by the Administration of its willingness to enter into unconditional discussions by all diplomatic means."

(By urging an extension of the holiday cease-fire, by demanding that the U.S. do "more" in the economic and political fields in South Vietnam, by defending the right of dissent and in stating that American forces should not stay in Vietnam any longer than necessary, Kennedy, according to some observers, sought throughout 1965 to create the impression that his views on the war were somehow different than those of Pres. Johnson, whose position he "basically supported.")

'Peace Offensive' & Bombing Halt

In the closing weeks of 1965, Pres. Johnson launched a "peace offensive." Leading American officials traveled to various world capitals to restate and seek support for U.S. policy while sounding out the possibilities of a negotiated settlement of the war.

The diplomatic flurry was accompanied by a pause in the bombings of North Vietnam that lasted from Dec. 24, 1965 to Jan. 31, 1966. An AP poll of 50 Senators willing to express their views showed Jan. 26 that 25 favored and 25 opposed a resumption of the bombings of North Vietnam. Robert Kennedy was included among those opposed to a resumption of the bombing.

Gen. Maxwell D. Taylor, a special adviser to Johnson, said Jan. 26, 1966 that the reasons for suspending the air raids had been "exhausted" and that, therefore, the bombings should be resumed. Speaking in New York at the annual luncheon of the Pilgrims of the United States, Taylor said that by halting the air attacks "we have shown friends and foes the sincerity of our peaceful purposes."

A letter calling for continued suspension of the air strikes was signed by 15 Democratic Senators and presented to Johnson Jan. 27. The message said: "We believe we understand in some small degree the agony you must suffer when called upon by our constitutional system to make judgments which may involve war or peace. We believe you should have our collective judgment before you when you make your decision." The letter had been drafted by Sens. Vance Hartke (Ind.), Eugene McCarthy (Minn.), George McGovern (S.D.), Quentin Burdick (N.D.), Lee Metcalf (Mont.) and Frank E. Moss (Utah). (Moss was in London and was unable to sign the letter.) The other signers were Sens. Edward L. Bartlett (Alaska), Maurine Neuberger (Ore.), Frank Church (Ida.), William Proxmire (Wis.), Stephen M. Young (O.), Joseph S. Clark (Pa.), Ernest Gruening (Alaska) and Harrison A. Williams Jr. (N.J.).

Sens. Robert and Edward Kennedy, Mike Mansfield (D., Mont.), J. William Fulbright (D., Ark.) and George D. Aiken (R., Vt.) did not sign the letter, although Fulbright and Aiken were cited in the text as being opposed to a resumption of the bombing, and Mansfield Jan. 24 had called for an "indefinite" suspension of the bombing. Robert Kennedy, in a statement of his own, did not state clearly whether the bombing should be resumed, but he cautioned, "If we regard bombing as the answer to Vietnam, we are heading straight to disaster."

The resumption of the U.S. bombings of North Vietnam Jan. 31, following a 37-day hiatus, was announced by Johnson in a radio-TV address broadcast several hours after the raids had been resumed. The President simultaneously instructed Amb.-to-UN Goldberg to ask the Security Council to intervene in the crisis and seek an international conference to end the war and establish peace in Southeast Asia.

RFK Neutral on Bombing

The decision to resume the bombing precipitated debate Jan. 31 in both houses of Congress. Kennedy neither denounced nor indorsed the decision to resume the bombing. Instead, he repeated his contention that bombing was not "the answer" and reiterated his long-held view that successful counter-insurgency required political as well as military initiatives. The political effort was lagging in South Vietnam, he complained. Discussing the resumption of the bombing, Kennedy said:

"The President has made his decision. In this time of crisis, he will have the support of Americans as he seeks an end to the tragic war in Vietnam. I welcome especially his announcement of new initiatives in the United Nations. But obviously the resumption of bombing in the North is not a policy. And we should not delude ourselves that it offers a painless method of winning the war. Our objectives in Vietnam can be gained only by what we do in the South—by what we do to show the people of that unhappy land that there is a difference—that this is their war—that the defeat of the Viet Cong will lead to a better life for themselves and their children. And there are many indications that we have not yet even begun to develop a program to make these objectives a reality....

"To such conditions, military action in the South or in the North is no answer. Military action is needed to allow social reform to take place. But if American soldiers are to fight and die to buy time for the government of South Vietnam, that time must be used. It is absolutely urgent that we now act to institute new programs of educational reform, public health, political participation—and that we act to insure honest administration. In my judgment, development and implementation of such a program would offer far more promise of achieving our aims in Vietnam than any other steps we could take—including the bombing of the North.

"As I have emphasized repeatedly, and I state again, our military effort will mean nothing if it is not followed by a successful pacification effort which inspires the people of South Vietnam. But we have not yet made the effort [that is] necessary. We are spending far more on military efforts than on all the education, land reform, and welfare programs which might convince a young South Vietnamese that his future is not best served by the Communists. And the best talent and brains in our government are focused far more on military action than they are on programs which might help the people of South Vietnam—and in the long run, help our effort as well.

"This imbalance must change. For if we regard bombing as the answer in Vietnam—we are headed straight for disaster. In the past, bombing has not proved a decisive weapon against a rural economy—or against a guerrilla army. And the temptation will now be to argue that if limited bombing does not produce a solution, that further bombing, more extended military action, is the answer. The danger is that the decision to resume may become the first in a series of steps on a road from which there is no turning back—a road which leads to catastrophe for all mankind. That cannot be permitted to happen.

"As we move into this new phase of the war, the President will need the support and encouragement of the American people. To be effective, however, both the Congress and the citizens of this country will have to be kept fully informed about the actions of the United States and the developments in Vietnam. I believe he will have this support even where there might be some differences of emphasis or policy. This should be clearly understood in both Hanoi and Peiping."

NEITHER HAWK NOR DOVE: FEB. 1966-FEB. 1967

RFK Proposes Coalition Government

Sen. Robert Kennedy broke temporarily with the Johnson Administration on Vietnam when he proposed at a Washington press conference Feb. 19, 1966 that the National Liberation Front (NLF), the Viet Cong's political arm, be "admit[ted] to a share of power and responsibility" in a future South Vietnamese coalition government "as part of a negotiated settlement of the Vietnamese war." The statement said nothing about U.S. bombings of North Vietnam.

Pres. Johnson had stated previously that "the Viet Cong would not have difficulty being represented and having their views represented [during peace talks] if for a moment Hanoi decided she wanted to cease aggression." The difference between Administration policy and Kennedy's position, as enunciated Feb. 19, was that, whereas the Administration was willing to consider NLF views, it would not do so until Hanoi "decided she wanted to cease aggression." Kennedy, on the other hand, insisted that North Vietnam could not be expected to withdraw from the war and "accept a settlement which leaves in the South a hostile government, dedicated to the final physical destruction of all Communist elements [in the South], refusing any economic cooperation with the North, dependent upon the continued presence of American military power." According to Kennedy, a "coalition government" supported by "international guarantees" should satisfy the U.S.' "one irreducible demand" (that South Vietnam not be surrendered to the North) and North Vietnam's "one irreducible demand" (that the current government in South Vietnam be replaced by a non-"hostile" regime).

In his statement Feb. 19 Kennedy said:

The creation of a suitable coalition government in South Vietnam "may come about through a single conference or many meetings or by a slow, undramatic process of gradual accommodation. It will require enormous skill and political wisdom to find the point at which participation does not bring domination or internal conquest..... *It may mean a compromise government fully acceptable to neither side.* It certainly means that we must take considerable risks in the expectation that social and economic success will weaken the appeal of communism—and that sharing the burden and the satisfaction of helping to guide a nation will attract hostile elements toward a solution which will preserve both the independence of their country and their new-found share of power. And we must be willing to face the uncertainties of election, and the possibility of an eventual vote on reunification. We must be prepared to think about what kind of relationship such a reunified country would have to the United States, to Communist China, to the Soviet Union.

"If we are willing to accept these uncertainties and run the risks—and if our adversaries are willing to submit their cause to the same arbitration, the same peaceful choice—then a settlement may be possible; and the other hazards, of widening conflict and devastation, may be ended. Of course, such a road toward solution must be protected from sudden violent upheaval. There must be international guarantees to back up agreement,

73

good faith and mutual self-interest. Foreign forces must be withdrawn, by balanced and verified stages. And we must insist that the political process go forward under the rigorous supervision of a trusted international body."

In presenting his views on a coalition government, Kennedy dismissed the possibility of a unilateral U.S. withdrawal: "For the United States to withdraw now, as I said last May, would be a repudiation of commitments undertaken and confirmed by 3 administrations. It would flatly betray those in Vietnam whom we have encouraged by our support to resist the forces of Hanoi and the Viet Cong. Unilateral withdrawal would injure, perhaps irreparably, the principle of collective security and undermine the independence of small nations everywhere in the world. And it would offer no hope for a reasonable accommodation with China in the future. There are reasonable and responsible steps which we can take to raise the possibility of improved relations with China in the future. But unilateral withdrawal would only reward aggression and could offer China no inducement to reach accommodation in a peaceful world."

Kennedy also said at his Feb. 19 press conference:

"...Abraham Lincoln was reviled for opposing the war of [1846-]1848. The citizens of his own state called Daniel Webster traitor for proposing a compromise to avoid civil war. Those who saw the storm, and tried desperately to prepare the nation for World War II, were cursed as warmongers, enemies of mankind, subverters of democracy—and worse. Yet despite the condemnations and the violent recriminations, there have always been within the Senate enough men of courage and conviction to triumph in the end over those who would stifle free discussion and action.

"There are hazards in debating American policy in the face of a stern and dangerous enemy. But that hazard is the essence of our democracy. Democracy is no easy form of government. Few nations have been able to sustain it. For it requires that we take the chances of freedom; that the liberating play of reason be brought to bear on events filled with passion; that dissent be allowed to make its appeal for acceptance; that men chance error in their search for the truth....

"Our constitution imposes on the Senate the most heavy and grave independent responsibilities. We ourselves owe to the people of 50 States the burden of independent thought and action. Our whole system of government rests on a complex structure...which requires that we make our own judgments about events, giving due weight to the reason and responsibility of others. Shall we then debate with force and passion the issues of labor relations and housing and trade—while the great issues of peace and war are allowed to pass in silence? Shall we discuss the standard of living of our constituents—while policies which affect their very existence go undiscussed? To do so would be the gravest departure from our duties as representatives of the people of the American states....

"The discussions which have been taking place in recent days are therefore worthwhile and important. But we must do all we can to make certain that the exchange of views accomplishes the most for our country—moving our policy toward the goals we all want to achieve.

"All of us are concerned, as the American people are concerned, about the progress of the struggle in Vietnam.... We are concerned at the casualties, the death and suffering, of our young men in South Vietnam. We are concerned over the effect of some of our military actions on the people of South Vietnam—whether more cannot be done to lessen the death and destruction of the innocent that comes with war. For a military victory at the cost of a completely destroyed South Vietnam would be a defeat for our larger purposes. We are concerned whether the people of South Vietnam are being offered something positive to live and fight for—something beyond negative anti-communism. The President's recent initiatives are to be applauded and welcomed; but it is now incumbent on the government of South Vietnam to make good at last on promises which the people of that unhappy country have heard for many years.

"We are concerned over our relationship with Communist China—not just concern to avoid a deadly war, but also concern lest the Vietnam struggle make any reasonable accommodation with China impossible in the future. The events of the coming decade will determine whether our relations with mainland China will change for the better or for the worse. But they will change and we can influence that change; and the direction of change must receive the earnest attention of the Senate.

"And we are concerned about the effect of the war on our domestic efforts to conquer ignorance and disease and unemployment—the problems of the cities—problems which, warned the McCone Commission, could split our society irretrievably. And this concern is heightened by the way in which the war perpetuates discrimination—for the poor and the less fortunate serve in Vietnam out of all proportion to their numbers in the United States as a whole.

"But the central question before us now—the area of greatest present concern for the Senate, and what we must discuss at all levels of government—is our political strategy in the war in Vietnam; not simply *how* to move, but in what direction we *wish* to move.

"At the outset, it must be realized that negotiations are not an ultimate goal. Negotiations or discussions are only a means by which ultimate goals may be reached. Our arrival at the bargaining table will not make the struggle disappear. Even if we arrive at the bargaining table, the real question is what goals we will seek there. Without clear goals in mind, negotiations are pointless. And without clear goals and realistic objectives, it is doubtful whether the bargaining table will ever be reached.

"What, then, are our goals in Vietnam? The Secretary of State and others have stated objectives in general terms. They are the independence of South Vietnam—or, at least, its independent right to determine its own future. They are to halt the aggression from the North and to prove to China that a policy of subversion in other lands will not work. These are worthy objectives. All are important. The question remains, however, under what realistic terms and conditions they can be advanced in Vietnam.

"There are 3 routes before us: military victory, a peaceful settlement, or withdrawal.

"The last is impossible for this country. For the United States to withdraw now, as I said last May, would be a repudiation of commitments undertaken and confirmed by 3 administrations. . . .

"I now turn to the open avenues—military victory or a peaceful settlement.

"Military victory requires that we crush both our adversary's strength and his will to continue the battle; that the forces from the North be compelled to withdraw beyond the border; that much of Vietnam be destroyed and its people killed; that we continue to occupy South Vietnam as long as our presence is required to insure that hostilities, including insurgency, will not be resumed. And this will be a very long time indeed. I cannot say with certainty that such an outcome is beyond our reach. We do know, however, that it would mean rapidly increasing commitments of American forces. It would mean a growing risk of widening war—with North Vietnam, with China, even with the Soviet Union. It would lead, indeed already has led, thoughtless people to advocate the use of nuclear weapons. And it would involve all these things—commitment, risk and spreading destruction—in pursuit of a goal which is at best uncertain, and at worst unattainable.

"Despite all these dangers, we may yet come to this course. The intransigence of our adversaries may leave us no alternative. There should be no misunderstanding or miscalculation of this point in either Hanoi or Peking. The American people possess the bravery and the will to follow such a course if others force it upon us. I also believe, however, that given the opportunity by our adversaries, we possess the wisdom, and skill to avoid such a grim necessity.

"And Pres. Johnson has made clear, on behalf of the United States, in every forum of the world, that this country seeks the other road: the road to negotiated settlement. In this pursuit we have asked for unconditional discussions. This means simply that we will neither demand nor yield specific formal commitments before bargaining begins. In fact, both sides must come to any discussion with at least one basic condition; one irreducible demand; one point they will not yield. For the United States it must be that we will not turn South Vietnam over to the North. For North Vietnam it must be that they will not accept a settlement which leaves in the South a hostile government, dedicated to the final physical destruction of all Communist elements, refusing any economic cooperation with the North, dependent upon the continued presence of American military power.

"These conditions, these minimum terms, can be breached only at sword's point, only by driving the adversary's forces from the field. For either side to yield its minimum conditions would be in fact to accept defeat. If we intend to deny these minimum conditions to our adversaries, then we must defeat them completely. If this is what we intend, we should understand it clearly—and undertake it with resolution.

"But if negotiation is our aim, as we have so clearly said it is, we must seek a middle ground. *A negotiated settlement means that each side must concede matters that are important in order to preserve positions that are essential.*

"It may be that negotiation is not possible in this war because our political aims are irreconcilable; because one side, or both sides, are not willing to accept anything less than the fruits of victory. If that is so, then we must reluctantly let slip the hope of reasoned discussion and proceed to the uncertain, uncharted course of war.

"I believe there is a middle way, that an end to the fighting and a peaceful settlement can be achieved.

"It must be said, before all else, that the middle way—the way of negotiation—involves risks. An adversary who lives may perhaps fight another day. And a government which is not continuously sheltered by American military power may be again attacked or subverted or overthrown. These risks, I believe, we are courageous enough to undertake. They are risks, in fact, which we do take every day in a hundred countries in every corner of every continent. There are dozens of countries which might be the target of Communist aggression or subversion. If we were unwilling to take any risk that they might be subverted or conquered by the Communists, we might simply have occupied all of them. But clearly, we would rather live with such risks than attempt to occupy these nations. We take these risks because we believe men and nations will not willingly choose to submit to other men from other lands.

"If we are wrong in this basic faith, then Vietnam will be but a flicker in the conflagration which is to come. But in Indonesia, in Algeria, and in the Central African Republic the Chinese have suffered enormous defeats—not because we are stronger or more skilled than they—not because we defeated them. They were defeated because the people of these lands preferred to run their affairs in their own way—and our faith was justified. This basic faith may not be borne out on every occasion in every land. But in the past when the question has been clearly presented, men have chosen independence and freedom.

"With this basic faith in the aspirations of man, what are the elements of a settlement in Vietnam? Whatever the exact status of the National Liberation Front—puppet or partly independent—any negotiated settlement must accept the fact that there are discontented elements in South Vietnam, Communist and non-Communist, who desire to change the existing political and economic system of the country. There are 3 things you can do with such groups: kill or repress them, turn the country over to them, or admit them to a share of power and responsibility. The first 2 are now possible only through force of arms. The last—to admit them to a share of power and responsibility—is at the heart of the hope for a negotiated settlement. It is not the easy way or the sure way.... It will take statesmanship willing to exploit the very real differences of ambition and intention and interest between Hanoi and Peking and the Soviet Union.... I would stress that such a settlement [resulting in a coalition government] would not end our burden or our vigilance in Vietnam. Pres. Johnson has made clear that we are ready to help with economic aid for North Vietnam. Further, if South Vietnam is to remain free to determine its own destiny and to live in harmony with the North, then we must help repair the ravages of 20 years of war. Our reconstruction effort may be nearly as costly, and more demanding of care and intelligence, than is our present military effort. And we must continue to stand guard against any violation of the agreement, which must make clear that the United States would not permit the country or the government to be seized by an outside power.

"There will be many other difficulties and problems.... We must have our terms set firmly in our own minds. And we must reveal enough of our intentions to Hanoi to eliminate any reasonable fear that we ask them to talk only to demand their surrender. And they must be given to understand as well that their present public demands are in fact a bid for us to surrender a vital national interest—but that, as a far larger and more powerful nation learned in October of 1962, surrender of a vital interest of the United States is an objective which cannot be achieved.

"I am aware that the United States cannot proclaim in advance the precise terms of an acceptable political settlement. We cannot show all our cards before we get to the bargaining table. Nor can we make all our concessions before receiving concessions from the other side. To so commit ourselves would be to show a weakness which could not serve the cause of justice or the cause of peace. But we ourselves must look at our own cards. And we must show enough of them to persuade our adversaries that a settlement is in their interests as well as our own.

"The Senate could serve no higher function than to discuss—for the benefit of our own people, for our adversaries, and for the people of the world—a framework within which a settlement would be acceptable. That is why discussion and debate in the Senate are now so important. We stand at the doorway of great decisions and fateful action. To decide in ignorance is to risk disaster. But if we now can clearly define our ends in South Vietnam, if we can at least begin discussing what our future relations with mainland China are to be, if we can adapt our means to those ends, *and, most important, if we can use only that force—and no more—that is needed to accomplish these objectives,* then there is hope that they may be achieved without prohibitive cost to ourselves, to the people of Vietnam, or to the peace of the world...."

Vice Pres. Hubert H. Humphrey, then on tour in Wellington, New Zealand, called a press conference at which he likened Kennedy's formula for a coalition government to "putting a fox in a chicken coup" or "an arsonist in a fire department."

Kennedy's proposals were criticized Feb. 20 by State Undersecy. George W. Ball and Presidential Assistant McGeorge Bundy. Appearing on the ABC-TV program "Issues and Answers," Ball said Kennedy's suggestion "would mean creating a coalition government in which the Communists, who are the hardcore elements trained in subversion, would move in with people politically who played no part in the present government, and what we would have would be only, in a very short time, a Communist government in Saigon." Bundy, on NBC-TV's "Meet the Press" program, attacked Kennedy's suggestion by quoting this statement made by the late Pres. John F. Kennedy in a speech in Berlin in 1963: "I am not impressed by the opportunities open to popular front throughout the world. I do not believe that any democrat can successfully ride that tiger." (Despite the statement cited by Bundy—or perhaps in an action that gave him cause to make the statement—Pres. Kennedy had accepted a coalition government in Laos in 1962.)

A bit surprised by the flurry of criticism directed at his speech, Kennedy returned from a skiing vacation to "clarify" his position. At the end of the week *Time* magazine and other publications accused him of having backed down and reversed himself.

Appearing Feb. 22 on NBC-TV's "Today" program, Kennedy said he had not proposed that the NLF be "automatically" included in a coalition government prior to elections. Kennedy said he had meant that the NLF should not be "automatically excluded" from a share of power. The question of the make-up of an interim government prior to elections, Kennedy suggested, should be settled at the negotiating table. Kennedy said he had gotten the impression from Administration leaders' statements that Washington's offer of "unconditional negotiations" actually contained the "preconditions" that the U.S. would not "abide by free elections" in Vietnam if the NLF won representation in a government. Kennedy said a refusal to grant the NLF representation won in balloting would lead to "a bloody, bloody war" because the South Vietnamese government controlled only "25% of the population." Kennedy said he thought the Administration displayed "confusion" in its stated positions.

The Johnson Administration's first official reaction to Kennedy's proposals was voiced Feb. 22 by White House Press Secy. Bill D. Moyers. Moyers said the Administration and Kennedy were in no disagreement "if Sen. Kennedy did not propose a coalition government with Communist participation before elections were held." Moyers said the Administration also agreed with Kennedy that the composition of a South Vietnamese government prior to elections "should be left to the negotiating parties." Moyers, however, denied Kennedy's contention of Administration "confusion" and the setting of preconditions. Citing testimony by State Secy. Dean Rusk before the Senate Foreign Relations Committee Feb. 18, Moyers said: The Administration was willing "to accept the decision of the people of Vietnam as expressed in a free election. We are for free elections with all of us abiding by the consequences of those elections, whatever they may be."

Kennedy said Feb. 22 that he had phoned Moyers and that they agreed that their views coincided.

Gen. Maxwell D. Taylor, a close Kennedy friend and adviser to Pres. Johnson, had said Feb. 21 that Kennedy's position was "very, very close to what I consider my position." In an interview with the *N.Y. Herald Tribune,* Taylor emphasized that he opposed the presence of Communists in a coalition government before elections. Taylor sought Feb. 22 to clarify this remark in view of his assertion to the Senate Foreign Relations Committee the previous week that he favored a settlement of the war along the 17th Parallel "if all the Viet Cong would go home and go north." In his clarification statement, Taylor said he favored "unconditional negotiations followed by free elections, with all of us abiding by the results.... The way to get there is through negotiations without setting any preconditions whatsoever."

J. W. Fulbright (D., Ark.) of the Senate Foreign Relations Committee Feb. 21 supported Kennedy's proposal and asserted that he favored giving the NLF "a share of power and responsibility" in a coalition government. He said he also backed Kennedy's view that the NLF should attend future peace talks as "an independent entity," not only as part of the North Vietnamese delegation.

Sen. Jacob K. Javits (R., N.Y.) Feb. 21 characterized Kennedy's proposal for inclusion of the NLF in a coalition regime as "a way-out suggestion" that would not lead to peace talks since North Vietnam had insisted that the NLF be given "a decisive role" in any new Saigon government. Javits came out for the NLF as an "independent negotiating party" at a peace conference. The composition of a future coalition government, Javits said, should be decided during negotiations and "should not be prejudged by any prior concessions."

Vice Pres. Humphrey and Kennedy Feb. 27 again expressed opposing views on the postwar role of the Viet Cong in a South Vietnamese government.

Appearing on the ABC-TV "Issues & Answers" program Feb. 27, Humphrey said: The Viet Cong "engage in assassination, murder, pillage, conquest, and I can't for the life of me see why the United States of America would want to propose that such an outfit be made part of any government." "If the people of South Vietnam wish to make that choice themselves," that would be a different matter, but he did not think it likely to happen.

Kennedy said Feb. 27 on the CBS-TV "Face the Nation" program: If U.S. policy was "realistic" and "candid," it would concede that the Communists "are going to end up, in some way or another, within the governmental structure of South Vietnam." Such a development would occur either in an interim government, prior to a general peace settlement, or in an elected government, dependent on the election results. If the Communists were barred in advance from the government, "then we really can't expect that they will come to the negotiating table." "I think that statements...that we will never deal with assassins or murderers make it difficult for them to believe that they are being asked to come to the negotiating table for anything other than to surrender."

A statement deploring the "feuding and posturing" by Humphrey and Kennedy over Vietnam policy was issued Feb. 27 by the Council of Republican Organizations, a group of liberal Republicans, The statement said the debate between the 2 men "contributed to national disunity" and jeopardized a peaceful resolution of the Vietnam conflict. It characterized the debate as "personal pronouncements designed to enhance the position of 2 obvious, yet undeclared, candidates" for President.

Kennedy Feb. 28 again sought to soften some of the hostile reaction to his proposal. In a speech before the Jewish Theological Seminary in Hollywood, Fla. Feb 28, he said: "All of us who participate now must keep in our minds and hearts that there are good men on all sides of the debate, that most of us share the same objectives about Vietnam. I made my statement about Vietnam a week ago Saturday in furtherance of these shared objectives: to help us reach a just negotiated settlement which preserves our essential national interests, and meets our essential commitment to the people of South Vietnam; to help bring the war to an early end; to thus save thousands of American lives; and to limit the destruction and devastation which war brings to the innocent people of South Vietnam."

In a 3-page interview published in *U.S. News and World Report* Mar. 14, 1966 Kennedy again "clarified" his formula for peace in Vietnam. "If we can defeat" the Communists in South Vietnam "without paying a great price, an overwhelming price, then that's what I'd like to do," he said. "But if we're going to have tremendous destruction to the people of Vietnam, including innocent civilian women and children; and if we're going to have tremendous—very, very, very high—casualties; and if we're going to take some of these other dangers, such as war with China and even beyond, then we get to the fact that—because of these dangers—we have to try, at least ... to negotiate. My judgment is, therefore, that the deaths, destruction and risks involved in trying to destroy the Viet Cong completely make a negotiated settlement advisable if it can be done honorably. It was my judgment that this was also the policy of the [Johnson] Administration."

Since the price of a military victory would be "overwhelming" in terms of human life and because a U.S. withdrawal "would be catastrophic for American interests"—and "so unacceptable that it hardly needs to be discussed"—Kennedy proposed (in the magazine interview) what he called a middle course. This would have the Communists agreeing to "lay down their arms and return the area and people now under their control to the central Government and to refrain from interfering with the freedom of the people of South Vietnam to determine their own destiny." They would do so in return for "a settlement that brings them into the government structure and society in South Vietnam." As envisioned by Kennedy, first there would be an "interim period" in which the Viet Cong "might play a role." Then their representatives would be permitted " a role in the future government" of South Vietnam if they won "popular support in the elections later on."

According to Kennedy, the key to a negotiated settlement was first to hurt the Communists "enough [for them] to know that they aren't going to win," and 2d to make them "feel there is enough reason for them to negotiate to make it worth their while." In discussing his proposals for a negotiated peace Kennedy said nothing about the U.S. bombings of North Vietnam.

3 months later, in a May 1966 newsletter to constituents, Kennedy defined the U.S. objective in Vietnam as "a settlement that will free the South Vietnamese from terror and intimidation and prevent the forcible takeover of their country by North Vietnam and the National Liberation Front."

Action in the Senate

Congress Mar. 1 authorized $4,807,750,000 in emergency funds for fiscal 1966 to finance the war. The House vote was 392-4, the Senate vote 93-2, Sens. Wayne Morse and Ernest Gruening dissenting.

Earlier Mar. 1, the Senate had voted 92-5 to reject (by tabling) Sen. Morse's amendment to repeal the 1964 "Gulf of Tonkin Resolution," a measure authorizing the President "to take all necessary steps, including the use of armed force" to assist South Vietnam in the defense of its freedom. Those who voted against tabling the resolution were Sens. J. William Fulbright, Morse, Gruening, Eugene J. McCarthy (D., Minn.) and Stephen M. Young (D., O.).

A bill appropriating $13,135,719,000 in fiscal 1966 was passed by a Senate vote of 87-2 Mar. 2. The dissenting votes were cast by Morse and Gruening.

Kennedy Apr. 27 assailed the Administration's stated policy of permitting "no sanctuary"—in Communist China or elsewhere—for planes attacking U.S. aircraft over North Vietnam. Speaking in the Senate Kennedy said: "The latest reports of clashes with advanced aircraft over North Vietnam must be viewed with the gravest concern. The Soviet Union had made these high-performance aircraft available to North Vietnam. We do not know who is flying the planes. We do not know where the planes are based—whether in North Vietnam or across the border in China. But the Secretary of State has said—and a State Department spokesman repeated yesterday—that there will be no sanctuary. Our planes will pursue hostile aircraft to wherever they go—even over the border of China—and that there is no sanctuary for Chinese bases. What is occurring in North Vietnam is escalation of the war by them or us. The fact is that we are inexorably involved.... What will be the Chinese response, if her territory is bombed or her airspace invaded? Will the Chinese seek to strike at our bases—in Vietnam, or Thailand, or aboard our aircraft carriers? And if they do, what then will our response be—further bombing? And if the scale of bombing increases, will China confine herself to air fighting—or will it send its troops to engage ours on the ground in South Vietnam or elsewhere?"

In his Apr. 27 Senate speech, Kennedy reiterated that the U.S. "must face the fact that there is no quick or easy answer to Vietnam." The U.S.' best efforts and talents should be used to encourage the South Vietnamese to "organize their society and government to continue the fight," he said. "Without a viable political structure in South Vietnam, the efforts and sacrifice of our fighting men will be wasted." Kennedy, who as yet had not spoken out against the bombing of North Vietnam, advised that "no military action in North Vietnam or China can create or contribute to the creation of such a political structure in South Vietnam."

U.S. Bombs Hanoi-Haiphong Area

American bombers began attacking fuel storage installations near the North Vietnamese cities of Hanoi and Haiphong June 29. The attacks, repeated on successive days, were reported to have destroyed a substantial portion of North Vietnam's fuel handling and storage facilities. The raids were the first in the immediate vicinity of the North Vietnamese capital and the country's major port city. They were considered a major escalation of the U.S. air war against North Vietnam. All prior attacks had been directed at objectives away from the 2 North Vietnamese population centers. Although an overwhelming majority of members of Congress of both parties were known to support the Administration's new action in Vietnam, many prominent members, particularly in the Senate, voiced fears that the expanded air raids would lead to a wider war and not to the conference table.

Sen. Mansfield said the bombings "may make the road to the negotiating table that much more difficult." Sen. Aiken (Vt.) said the new raids would expand the war, not "shorten it." Aiken said Pres. Johnson was "apparently taking the advice of the same people who assured him 18 months ago that a few days bombing of North Vietnam would bring the Communists to the negotiating table." "They were wrong then," Aiken said.

Kennedy, meanwhile, continued his basic policy of supporting the war but neither indorsing nor criticizing the bombing of North Vietnam. Meanwhile, he sought to dissociate himself from Administration policies by urging greater political action in the South and insisting that bombing the North was not the key to winning the war in the South. In keeping with that policy, Kennedy, following the Hanoi-Haiphong bombings, asked only whether the extension of the bombing would "effectively prevent" North Vietnam from supplying the Viet Cong in South Vietnam. His Senate office issued this statement June 30:

"I am sure that all Americans are concerned at this expansion of the war in Vietnam. It seems to me that the major question to be answered with respect to the bombings is this: Will this step effectively prevent North Vietnam from supplying the Viet Cong in the South with sufficient men and material to enable them to continue the war at levels they desire? Unfortunately, past escalations have often been accompanied by assurances and predictions that this would be the case. These hopes have not been fulfilled. Had these predictions been correct, the bombings announced today would not have been necessary. Indeed, on each occasion the effort from the North has either increased in spite of our efforts, or taken a different and more dangerous course. I regret that it has seemed necessary to take this step. We must all hope that the predictions based on this latest heightening of the battle will prove to be realistic ones."

For the rest of 1966 Kennedy said little about Vietnam. During that period U.S. bombings of North Vietnam were intensified and U.S. troop strength in Vietnam was increased to some 350,000 men, 150,000 more than at the end of 1965. Opposition to the war intensified in Congress and became widespread throughout the country, where it was expressed in forms ranging from orderly demonstrations and the adoption of resolutions to draft card burnings and the shouting down of Administration spokesmen. In the autumn Kennedy campaigned extensively for Democratic candidates while steadfastly refusing to discuss the war. When questioned about it, he would merely cite the complexity of the problem or acknowledge that he had "reservations" about Administration policy. The *Wall Street Journal* noted Oct. 17: "Actually, Mr. Kennedy has been careful of late to avoid sharp attacks on the President. When he expresses doubts about Vietnam policy he always stresses that 'these are very complex problems, with no simple solutions.'"

West European Tour, No 'Peace Signal'

Robert Kennedy made a hurried tour of West European capitals Jan. 28-Feb. 5, 1967. In Britain Jan. 28, Kennedy addressed 1,000 members of the Oxford Union debating society in Oxford and expressed support for Pres. Johnson's policies on Vietnam. Kennedy said the Johnson Administration favored a solution that would permit the Vietnamese people "to choose any kind of government they want. If the people of South Vietnam want the Commies, Pres. Johnson has said he would abide by the results." Kennedy was quoted as saying secret talks to end the war were in progress and that the following 3 or 4 weeks would be "critical and crucial."

Kennedy clarified his Jan. 28 statement on arriving in Paris Jan. 29. He denied having said secret talks were going on. He explained that he was referring to meetings that were known to the public:

Soviet Premier Aleksei N. Kosygin's forthcoming visit to Britain, U.S.-Viet Cong contacts on prisoners of war and peace contacts by 3d parties. Because of those discussions, "the next few weeks will be critical and crucial," he said.

Kennedy met in Paris with French Foreign Min. Maurice Couve de Murville Jan 30 and spent 70 minutes Jan. 31 with French Pres. Charles de Gaulle, a leading critic of U.S. Vietnam policies. Kennedy said after his meeting with de Gaulle: "France and Gen. de Gaulle are going to play an important role in any successful effort we undertake to find a solution to the trouble in Vietnam. If that's not recognized in Washington, we are in great trouble."

Kennedy went to the Quai d'Orsay Feb. 1 to discuss Vietnam with Etienne Manac'h, director of Far East Affairs in the French Foreign Ministry. Kennedy was accompanied by John Gunther Dean, a first secretary in the American embassy in Paris. This meeting took place after Wilfred G. Burchett, an Australian journalist sympathetic to the Viet Cong and North Vietnamese and with good connections in Hanoi, had filed (in late January) a number of dispatches indicating that Hanoi was prepared to talk peace provided that the U.S. stopped bombing North Vietnam. Hanoi radio said Jan. 28 that North Vietnamese Foreign Min. Nguyen Duy Trinh had granted an interview to Burchett and had told Burchett that if the U.S. "really wants talks, it must first halt unconditionally the bombing raids and all other acts of war against the Democratic Republic of Vietnam." Previously, North Vietnam had said it would not negotiate with the U.S. Mai Van Bo, chief of the North Vietnamese mission in Paris, told Manac'h that Trinh's message was significant and serious.

Manac'h relayed Bo's observation to Dean in Kennedy's presence. Following his meeting with Kennedy and Manac'h, Dean cabled Manac'h's message to the State Department. A State Department official in Washington leaked the information to *Newsweek,* which reported that Kennedy had received a "peace signal" from Hanoi while in Paris.

The White House immediately assumed that Kennedy had provided the information to *Newsweek* to embarrass Pres. Johnson. Sensing this Kennedy arranged for an appointment at the White House with Johnson Feb. 6. Kennedy denied that he had given any information to *Newsweek,* and he urged Johnson to test Hanoi by stopping the bombings. The meeting grew heated and at one point Johnson reportedly told Kennedy that "we are going to win this war, and in 6 months all you doves will be finished." *Time* magazine asserted that Kennedy called the President "you SOB." Among those at the meeting were White House aid Walt W. Rostow and Undersecretary of State Nicholas deB. Katzenbach.

After his meeting with the President, Kennedy denied publicly that, while in Paris, he had received a North Vietnamese proposal for ending the war. Kennedy said: "I did not bring home any peace feelers. I never received the impression in any of the conversations" during his European tour "that I was the recipient of any peace feelers."

On his return to the U.S. Feb. 5, Kennedy had said in an airport statement in New York that U.S. participation in the Vietnamese war had resulted in an "undermining of United States prestige" in Europe. Kennedy said that because of the war and de Gaulle's attempts to undercut U.S. influence in Europe, the relations of European nations "to each other and the United States are quite different than they were 3 years ago.... Our influence is diminishing."

ROBERT KENNEDY AS DOVE: 1967-8

Sen. Kennedy joined the vocal opposition to Pres. Johnson's Vietnam policies in Feb. 1967, one month after his heated Jan. 6 exchange with Pres. Johnson at the White House.

The U.S. had suspended bombing attacks on North Vietnam Feb. 8-12 during the *Tet* (lunar new year) truce and for 2 days beyond the expiration of the truce, but the air raids were resumed Feb. 13. The resumption of the bombing evoked critical comment from Kennedy, who declared in a statement issued Feb. 13: "I deeply regret that the bombing of North Vietnam has resumed. Beyond that, it is most unfortunate that the truce period has gone by without greater progress being made by all of us on both sides toward a peaceful ending of this tragic war."

In explaining his decision to resume the bombings, Johnson said in a prepared statement issued Feb. 13: "It had been our hope that the truce periods connected with Christmas, New Year's and *Tet* might lead to some abatement of hostilities and to moves toward peace. Unfortunately, the only response we have had from the Hanoi government was to use the periods for major resupply efforts of their troops in South Vietnam. Despite our efforts and those of 3d parties, no other response has yet come from Hanoi. Under these circumstances, in fairness to our troops and those of our allies, we had no alternative but to resume full-scale hostilities after the cease-fire period." Johnson asserted, however, that "the door [to peace negotiations] is open and will remain open, and we are prepared at any time to go more than halfway to meet any equitable overture from the other side."

(A U.S. State Department official confirmed Feb. 11 that the U.S. also had continued to supply its forces in South Vietnam during the truce. The official justified the U.S. build-up on the grounds that the North Vietnamese violation of the cease-fire was "clear evidence of their intent to continue their aggressive action," while the U.S. was committed to counter aggression. U.S. Air Force officials in Saigon reported Feb. 11 that U.S. cargo planes had delivered a one-day record 2,762 tons of equipment to U.S. troops in the field Feb. 8. During the Feb. 8-10 period, U.S. planes had carried 7,042 tons of equipment and delivered more than 17,000 troops, the Air Force said.)

'Toward a China Policy'

Kennedy delivered a major speech, "Toward a China Policy," Feb. 8 at a conference on China at the University of Chicago. The speech contained several references to Vietnam, including the assertion that the war in Vietnam was not inspired by Communist China. He also questioned the extent and the nature of the U.S. commitment to South Vietnam. Kennedy said in his speech:

"If our common understanding of Chinese capabilities has been exaggerated, so has our common understanding of her potential as a source of revolution elsewhere. China's revolutionary experience is unique; and it is clear also that the revolutionary credo that accompanied it is not readily transferable to other nations.... There are sometimes attempts to portray Vietnam as a Chinese-inspired conflict, and China is assisting the North Vietnamese. But Vietnam's communism is basically a native growth, with its own revolutionary traditions and dynamism. There is always a potential danger to which we must be alert, but as of 1967 there is not one example, anywhere in the world, of Chinese-inspired or-directed revolution that has had any lasting success. ... [Only the Malayan revolt had] even the most minimal success, before being crushed, and that was carried out not by native Malayans but by ethnic Chinese. The record of Chinese effort to export revolution has been one of consistent, dramatic failure....

"Of course, we want to prevent the expansion, the acquisition of vast new resources, by powers deeply hostile to the United States. ... [But] how do we discriminate between Chinese expansion and autonomous revolt? Where and under what circumstances can we bring our power effectively to bear? Where and under what circumstances should we limit ourselves to helping others, without hazarding large-scale combat or major war? These are not easy questions to answer. But until we at least begin to discuss and debate them we will be unable to develop any kind of long-range planning, let alone policy. Even then, the application of that policy in any given situation may be painfully difficult."

The "self-righteous assertion of sweeping moral principles" was a corrupting "substitute for policy." "Blanket moral statements cannot determine all strategic judgments, and... their enunciation does not constitute a policy." Take for example the "blanket formulation—that we must keep our commitments or meet our obligations. By what standards, and toward what ends, are those commitments made? How deeply do they extend, and what means will be used to fulfill them? Thus it is one thing to defend a commitment in Vietnam; yet it is something else indeed to fulfill that commitment by extending military operations to Thailand, in return making a new commitment to that nation as well. What is to govern the form of the commitment—whether it is to be a commitment to help others help themselves, or a commitment to ensure victory whether they help themselves or not? When we make the first, do we slowly and inexorably and almost automatically accept the latter?"

War Blamed for Disaffection of Youth

Speaking at a dinner Feb. 24 sponsored by the Americans for Democratic Action, Kennedy called the war in Vietnam a major cause of student unrest. "When a hundred student-body presidents and editors of college newspapers, hundreds of former Peace Corps volunteers, dozens of present Rhodes Scholars question the basic premises of the war, they should not and cannot be ignored," he declared. Kennedy said:

"These students oppose the war for the brutality and the horror of all wars, and for the particular terror of this one. But for our young people, I suspect, Vietnam is a shock as it cannot be to us. They did not know World War II, or even Korea. And this is a war surrounded by rhetoric they do not understand or accept; these are the children not of the cold war, but of the thaw. Their memories of communism are not of Stalin's purges and death camps, not even the terrible revelations of the 20th [Soviet Communist] Party Congress, or the streets of Hungary. They see the world as one in which Communist states can be each others' deadliest enemies or even friends of the West, in which communism is certainly no better, but perhaps no worse, than many other evil and repressive dictatorships all around the world—with which we conclude alliances when that is felt to be in our interest...."

"We speak of past commitments, of the burden of past mistakes; and they ask why they should now atone for mistakes made before many of them were born, before almost any could vote. They see us spend billions on armaments while poverty and ignorance continue at home; they see us willing to fight a war for freedom in Vietnam, but unwilling to fight with 1/100 the money or force or effort to secure freedom in Mississippi or Alabama or the ghettos of the North. And they see, perhaps most disturbing of all, that they are remote from the decisions of policy; that they themselves frequently do not, by the nature of our political system, share in the power of choice on great questions shaping their lives."

Kennedy acknowledged, however, that all students did not oppose the war, that "there are others, as I have seen on many campuses, who are in favor of escalation—though many who favor escalation also favor continuation of the student deferment, their seeming slogan: 'Escalation without participation.'"

RFK Urges Bomb Halt, Confesses Errors

In his first major address against the war, in the Senate Mar. 2, 1967, Kennedy proposed a halt in the bombing of North Vietnam to get Hanoi to negotiate. For the first time, he blamed himself and Pres. Kennedy for faulty decisions on Vietnam. (As of Jan. 1971 Robert Kennedy was the only major official in either Democratic administration who admitted publicly to being wrong about Vietnam.)

"Nearly all Americans share with us the determination and intention to remain in Vietnam until we have fulfilled our commitments," Kennedy said. "There is no danger of any division—in this chamber or in this country—now or in the future—which will erode American will and compel American withdrawal. Nor are we here to curse the past or to praise it. 3 Presidents have taken action in Vietnam. As one who was involved in many of those decisions, I can testify that if fault is to be found or responsibility assessed, there is enough to go around for all—including myself."

Kennedy described the horrors of the war. The war, he said, was "the vacant moment of amazed fear as a mother and child watch death by fire fall from the improbable machine sent by a country they barely comprehend. It is the sudden terror of the official or the civil guard absorbed in the work of his village as he realizes the Viet Cong assassin is about to take his life. It is the refugees wandering, homeless, from villages now obliterated, leaving behind only those who did not live to flee. It is the young men, Vietnamese and American, who in an instant sense the night of death destroying yesterday's promise of family and land and home.... The mounting devastation of South Vietnam—the destruction of villages and burning of the countryside—is steadily eroding the fabric of that society."

Kennedy put most of the blame for the continued fighting on the enemy: "The fault rests largely with our adversary. He has pursued relentless and unyielding conquest with obdurate unconcern for mounting desolation." Yet, Americans must be certain "that there is nothing we have left undone which might have been done" to bring about peace, he declared.

Therefore, Kennedy said, "I propose that we test the sincerity of the statements by [Soviet] Premier [Aleksei] Kosygin and others asserting that if the bombardment of the North is halted, negotiations would begin—by halting the bombardment and saying we are ready to negotiate within the week, making it clear that discussions cannot continue for a prolonged period without an agreement that neither side will substantially increase the size of the war in Vietnam—by infiltration or reinforcement. An international group should be asked to inspect the borders and ports of the country to report any further escalation."

"If the passage of substantial time and events proves that our adversaries do not sincerely seek a negotiated solution," Kennedy continued, "if discussions are used only as a pretext to enlarge the conflict in the South, then we can reexamine our entire military strategy—including the bombing or the possible erection of a physical barrier to block infiltration...."

"Suspension of the bombing might be more difficult if continued bombing of North Vietnam were a promising and indispensable way to secure our objectives in South Vietnam," Kennedy declared. But that is not the case, he said. "It should be clear by now that the bombardment of the North cannot bring an end to the war in the South.... Certainly the bombing of the North makes the war more costly and difficult and painful for North Vietnam. It is harsh punishment indeed. But we are not in Vietnam to play the role of an avenging angel pouring death and destruction on the roads and factories and homes of a guilty land."

Kennedy concluded by outlining a possible political settlement of the war that centered on the establishment of a freely elected civilian South Vietnamese government that would seek a negotiated settlement with the Communists. "Once a civilian government has been freely chosen," he said, "South Vietnam will be in the hands of its own people, subject to the uncertainties, risks and promise of the political process in a turbulent land."

In his Mar. 2 speech, Kennedy also said:

"... If our enemy will not accept peace, it cannot come. Yet, we must also look to ourselves. We must have no doubt that it is not our acts or failures which bar the way.... Our own course must be subject to a ceaseless and critical examination, not with certainty that change will bring success, but in order that our own people can take comfort and strength from the knowledge that America has taken every step, done every act, and performed every deed within its power to put an end to this distant and ferocious war. For if this war was not our doing, and is not our fault, still it is partly our responsibility. Events, many of them beyond our control, have brought the astounding might of American power upon a remote and alien people in a small and unknown land. It is difficult to feel in our hearts what this war means to the people of Vietnam. It is on the other side of the world and its people are strangers. Few of us are directly involved while the rest of us continue our lives and pursue our ambitions undisturbed by the sounds and fears of battle....

"It is a country where hundreds of thousands fight, but millions more are the innocent, bewildered victims of brutal passions and beliefs they barely understand. To them peace is not an abstract term describing one of those infrequent intervals when men are not killing each other, it is a day without terror and the fall of bombs. ...

"All we say and all we do must be informed by our awareness that this horror is partly our responsibility; not just a nation's responsibility, but yours and mine. It is we who live in abundance and send our young men out to die. It is our chemicals that scorch the children and our bombs that level the villages. We are all participants. To know this, and to feel the burden of this responsibility, is not to ignore important interests, nor to forget that freedom and security must, at times, be paid for in blood. Still even though we must know, as a nation, what it is necessary to do, we must also feel, as men, the anguish of what it is we are doing.

"Of course power is the instrument of war and devastation the product of power; although restraint in power's use can blend wisdom with compassion. Many such restraints have been carefully imposed by the President. Nor would I contend that the pain and death of conflict alone impel us to a swift settlement. It is not necessarily merciful nor wise to purchase a temporary respite at the price of a future disaster.

"Yet our apprehension of this war's agony now joins with other mounting urgencies to command us to seek every opportunity, open every door, and tread every path which may lead to the end of the war.

"We are now steadily widening the war in order, we are told, to increase the costs to Hanoi. Yet, in our concern with the price our adversary must pay, let us not omit our own costs from the war's account. The mounting devastation of South Vietnam—the destruction of villages and burning of the countryside—is steadily eroding the fabric of that society; making the ultimate reconstruction of South Vietnam more remote and difficult. Yet, lasting peace depends upon the strength of the nation we leave behind. The war has also made far more difficult the hopeful pursuit of fresh understanding and diminishing tension between the 2 great nuclear powers: the United States and the Soviet Union. It has absorbed some of the energies needed if we are to exercise our full weight and responsibility in the Western Alliance. It is diverting resources which might have been used to help eliminate American poverty, improve the education of our children and enhance the quality of our national life.

"Of course we are willing—we must be willing—to pay all these costs if the alternative is surrender or defeat. We cannot dishonor our commitments nor yield the lawful interests of the nation at any price. But neither should we deceive ourselves into thinking these are not massive and difficult debts which other generations will have to discharge.

"The destruction and costs of this war are borne in pursuit of what [Defense] Secy. [Robert] McNamara has called limited objectives—not conquest or alliance, but the protection of South Vietnam from domination by force. It is an objective which, our government has always said, can best be achieved at the conference table. For years, Pres. Johnson has dedicated his energies in an effort to achieve an honorable peace.

"However, we are now at a critical turning point in pursuit of our stated limited objectives: balanced between the rising prospects of peace and surely rising war, between the promise of negotiations and the perils of spreading conflict. For our attacks are mounting in intensity, just as the evidence mounts that a new, and more hopeful moment of opportunity for settlement has been at hand.

"Before reawakened hope is lost in renewed and ever more far-reaching assaults, we should test this moment with new initiatives and acts in pursuit of peaceful settlement.... As our objectives are limited, they may well be secured at the conference table without further months or years of war. If our effort fails, then the conflict will continue....

"We need not wait timidly for a certain outcome and sure guarantees, fearful for our dignity and anxious for our prestige. This enormous country, a nation which commands half the wealth and power of the globe, need not be fearful of North Vietnam. Viet Cong guerrillas, even with their northern allies, will not drive from the battlefield an American army, backed by endless funds and towering resources. No one is going to defeat us, or slaughter our troops, or destroy our prestige, because we dare take initiatives for peace. If Pope Paul or U Thant or [British] Prime Min. [Harold] Wilson or [Soviet] Premier [Aleksei] Kosygin believe they have the key to peace, let us welcome their efforts and continuously ask their help. If any among us can suggest any act which offers hope of peace, let his counsel be welcomed. 'Where no counsel is' the bible says, 'the people fall: but in the multitude of counselors there is safety.'...

"Our government has unequivocally said that our objective in Vietnam is a negotiated settlement with the Communists. 'The only path for reasonable men,' Pres. Johnson said at Johns Hopkins, 'is the path of peaceful settlement.'... The question is whether we are doing everything possible to reach that goal....

"The steps I am suggesting are intimately related. They stand together, each dependent on the other. It will do little good to go to the conference table if discussions are simply used to mask continued escalation of the war. Nor will negotiations be fruitful unless they lead to a reasonable and honorable settlement with some hope of lasting peace. Therefore, I propose that we test the sincerity of the statements by Premier Kosygin and others asserting that if the bombardment of the North is halted, negotiations would begin—by halting the bombardment and saying we are ready to negotiate within the week.... And under the directions of the United Nations, and with an international presence gradually replacing American forces, we should move toward a final settlement which allows all the major political elements in South Vietnam to participate in the choice of leadership and shape their future direction as a people.

"If we can follow this course, we cannot be certain that negotiations will take place, or that they will be productive. ... But measures such as these will enhance the chances of peace while the risks are comparatively slight....

"There are 3 stages toward final resolution of the war in Vietnam: beginning negotiations, continuing those discussions without increasing conflict, and a final settlement which liberates the people of South Vietnam to govern their own future.

"First, we must get to the negotiating table. For almost 2 years we have proclaimed and published our unwavering desire to begin negotiations with our Communist enemy. ... Last year we unilaterally stopped the bombing of North Vietnam for 37 days without asking any prior act, signal or statement in return, hoping our restraint might bring negotiations. Now the evidence is mounting that our initiative can finally bring the negotiations we have sought for so long if only we are willing to do what we did before.

"2 weeks ago in London, Mr. Kosygin, the premier of the Soviet Union, the principal ally of North Vietnam, said that the first step toward peace 'should be the unconditional cessation of the bombing of, and all other aggressive acts against, North Vietnam. As the foreign minister of North Vietnam declared recently, this step is necessary to enable talks between North Vietnam and the United States to take place. The Soviet government welcomes this statement and regards it as an important and constructive proposal for ending the war.'

"This declaration comes from a man of enormous authority in the Communist world, whose country helps sustain North Vietnam's effort. It does not demand that we withdraw our forces, slow down our military effort on the ground, or even halt the bombing of South Vietnam. It does not demand an indissoluble and binding guarantee that we will never use our planes again at any future time no matter what our adversary does to enlarge his effort or change the nature of the war. Demands and replies must be understood in the context of the present situation, not a drastically different one which may or may not be created in the future by our adversary. There is no longer a demand that we accept any terms or conditions, such as the 4 Points, in advance of talks. We are simply informed that 'to enable talks' we should stop bombing—something we have done before.

"The same message has come to us in recent weeks from friends and adversaries alike, in public interviews and private communications. It was repeated again this week in a statement by Soviet Pres. [Nikolai] Podgorny, and again yesterday by the foreign minister of North Vietnam. Often the statements are more obscure than that of Mr. Kosygin. Some have been conflicting. Yet the temper of attitudes and events has been changing and we should reach for the moment of promise which may have come....

"Let us ... accept the public declarations of Mr. Kosygin and Mr. Podgorny—which in this respect were identical to the counsel offered us by Secy. Gen. U Thant. Let us halt the bombing and bombardment of the North as a step toward a negotiated peace, and say to Mr. Kosygin, to the National Liberation Front and to Hanoi, that we are ready to begin discussions within the week. This does not mean that we can expect a response with equal speed—only that we ourselves must be ready. There are many parties among our adversaries, some with different interests, which perhaps must be sorted out before negotiations can take place. After so many years of conflict and mutual distrust, it will require patience and severance and time to achieve peaceful settlement—if indeed, it is possible at all. But it may be possible.

"So let us place on the Soviet Union, on North Vietnam, the obligation to demonstrate the sincerity of their declarations by coming to the conference table. If their statements and our hopes are founded in reality, discussions may begin. If not, we will have proven to ourselves and our friends around the world that we are willing to take the initiative for peace; that it is our adversary, not America, that bars the way.

"We were willing to do this a year ago, even without the evidence we now have that an end to bombing attacks on the North may well bring negotiations. A year ago it was our adversaries who publicly laid down conditions for negotiations—acceptance of the 4 Points or withdrawal of American troops. Now Mr. Kosygin and Mr. Podgorny have said negotiation can begin on terms we clearly would have accepted then. Why then do we not try again in this far more hopeful moment?

"If the passage of substantial time and events proves that our adversaries do not sincerely seek a negotiated solution, if discussions are used only as a pretext to enlarge the conflict in the South, then we can reexamine our entire military strategy ... in light of the changing nature of the war. Our actions at that time, after such a dedicated effort to secure peace, would have the increased understanding and support of our allies and of our own people. We should be generous in our search for peace, but I am also aware of the precedent of Panmunjom....

"... The bombing of the North can be stopped as a step toward peace without effectively weakening our position in the South; especially when it is remembered that such a cessation would not affect our attacks on the infiltration trails in Laos or on enemy forces in the South. Pres. Johnson told us ... that we began bombing North Vietnam in 1965 for 3 purposes: The first was 'to increase the confidence of the brave people of South Vietnam'—assuring them they would not be abandoned. The bombing did help give such assurance. Now, however, we have 400,000 fighting men in the South, a far more effective and continuing proof of our commitment and determination. 2d, in the President's words: 'We wanted to convince the leaders of North Vietnam ... [that] we will not be defeated. We will not grow tired. We will not withdraw.' That purpose is also served by the enormous commitment of men, lives, and resources which we have made.... If our adversary has seen his hopes for victory destroyed, it is primarily because of the skill and bravery of our forces on the ground. Moreover, there is every sign that the bombing itself is now an insuperable obstacle to negotiations and that the North Vietnamese feel it impossible to discuss peace while bombs are falling on their country.... The 3d purpose, the President said, was 'to slow down aggression.' The bombing of the North would, it was hoped, reduce the flow of men and supplies from North Vietnam to the Communist forces in the South. A year ago, Gen. [Matthew B.] Ridgway—the commander of our last ground war in Asia—predicted that air attacks could not stop the infiltration of men and supplies through the scattered jungles, trails, and hills of Southeast Asia.... Although asserting that the bombing has other values which he supports, the Secretary of Defense [McNamara] has recently confirmed this prediction, testifying that although the bombing has punished the North and encouraged the South: 'I don't believe the bombing up to the present has significantly reduced, nor any bombing that I would contemplate in the future would significantly reduce, the actual flow of men and materials to the South.'...

"As soon as we halt the bombing of the North, international teams under the United Nations or, perhaps, a strengthened International Control Commission, should be asked to provide detached and objective information to the world about any large buildup of troops or supplies by our adversaries. They would patrol the borders, ports and roads of Vietnam....

"Our next step should be to seek an understanding with our adversaries that neither side will substantially increase the rate of infiltration and reinforcements during negotiations. For even though we begin negotiations it is not likely that peace can be discussed effectively or with confidence while the other side is preparing for a larger war. It is unrealistic to think we would sit through prolonged and fruitless negotiations while casualties mount and the war gets bigger. Thus, even if hostilities continue it will be necessary for both sides to refrain from escalating the war on the ground and trying to change the military balance....

"3d, we must know and clearly state what kind of Vietnam we would like to see emerge from negotiations and how we propose these general objectives could be best achieved. Negotiations are not the end of the road. They are the bridge to the future of South Vietnam. That future must include the right of the people of South Vietnam to self-determination. How to accomplish this is at the heart of the problem of peaceful settlement....

"As I said a year ago, a negotiated settlement is a compromise. One must either defeat an enemy and compel his surrender or else settle on terms in which both sides can find some degree of satisfaction. We have not defeated the Viet Cong, nor, as Pres. Johnson said in his State-of-the-Union message, is a military victory in sight. We must, therefore, find— and I think we can find—an agreed solution which, however imperfect, protects our basic interest in Vietnam: The self-determination of the people of South Vietnam. All the people of South Vietnam, Communist and non-Communist, Buddhist and Christian, should be able to choose their leaders, and seek office through peaceful political processes, free from external coercion and internal violence. All should have the opportunity to seek peacefully a share of power and responsibility through free elections. They should determine their future and the nature of their system and resolve the question of Vietnamese reunification.

"We might begin moving toward this future by encouraging the South Vietnamese government, including the present Constituent Assembly, to begin its own discussion with the National Liberation Front. Other political elements, not now represented in the government, should share in this effort. For many years the people of South Vietnam have been divided in fierce and hostile combat. If they are to settle their own future they must at least begin to talk to each other, try to eliminate unnecessary conflicts, and search out areas of possible agreement.

"And as a major combatant, we must also be ready to talk directly to all parties— North and South, Communist and non-Communist alike.

"However, if we want non-Communist Vietnamese to take a major role in discussions leading to a negotiated settlement—as I believe essential—and to exert effective force and influence in competition with the NFL for future leadership, we must first encourage a free political process among non-Communist South Vietnamese. The military directory is not representative of many of the non-Communist political elements in South Vietnam. Even the Assembly, a significant step toward civilian rule, excludes important elements of the population and, though it has taken positions independent of the military, is still far weaker than the generals. Thus the forthcoming elections, if conducted freely and fairly, could result in a civilian government, far more effective than the military rule which exists at present—one willing and able to take effective part in a negotiated settlement. We should begin now to help bring this about. And obviously, for a civilian government to be effective, it must engage in far more serious efforts at political and social reform than has any in the past. . . .

"Finally, a lasting settlement of the war will be extremely difficult unless all parties to the present conflict are secure in the knowledge that free elections open to all will ultimately be held, and that those who win them will take office. This confidence will depend on the structure of government between the end of hostilities and elections. . . . Therefore, the rights of all major political elements must be protected by any interim governing assembly. That, however, is not enough; suspicion and fear are now too deeply ingrained. The Communists would fear a takeover by the military, just as we might fear a Communist coup. Therefore it will be necessary to phase out the withdrawal of American and North Vietnamese forces over a period of time and, as our forces depart, to replace them by international forces to police the cease-fire, guard against violence and coercion, and supervise the elections. In this we can create the confidence necessary to agreement. . . .

"Once a civilian government has been freely chosen, . . . we can be hopeful that [South Vietnam] will reestablish friendly relations and commerce with the other countries with whom it shares Southeast Asia. Indeed, its relationship with North Vietnam, and that of the North with other countries, is critical to any lasting settlement of the conflicts in that volatile area.

"For even though the war in Vietnam has its unique difficulties and dangers, its resolution must be viewed against the shifting nature of world communism. In the '40s and '50s communism everywhere was guided from a single center. Communist parties in every land took their orders from Moscow. A Communist victory anywhere meant an automatic extension of the influence and power of the Soviet Union.

"There is still grave danger, but the monolithic Communist system is forever shattered. . . . A Communist state can no longer be assumed to be the automatically obedient instrument of expanding Russian or Chinese power. North Vietnam . . . can be encouraged to assert its own independence.

"We should, therefore, help to demonstrate the rich possibilities open to all of Vietnam and, indeed, to all Southeast Asia once steps are taken down the road to peace. In particular, we must show that peace can lead immediately to an increase in trade and communications between North Vietnam and its neighbors. We must show, perhaps in conjunction with the Soviet Union, that the security and economic welfare of North Vietnam are not in danger. And of great significance, it may be that in such a context North Vietnam will be better able to increase its independence of China. . . .

"In this way the settlement in South Vietnam may become a bridge to a solution for all Southeast Asia. And perhaps from today's terrible violence can come, not only an end to conflict, but also a decisive movement toward that liberation from misery and fear which is necessary to bring fruitful tranquillity to the nations and people of Southeast Asia. . . ."

After his Mar. 2 speech Kennedy asserted during an exchange with Sen. Frank Lausche (D., O.) that North Vietnam had come "all the way around and said we'll talk if you'll stop the bombing." Lausche had said he questioned the feasibility of Kennedy's proposal for a bombing pause in view of the fact that previous American bombing halts had not brought Hanoi to the conference table.

In a statement issued immediately after Kennedy's address, State Secy. Dean Rusk noted that "proposals substantially similar to those put forward by Sen. Kennedy were explored prior, during and since the [Feb. 8-12] *Tet* truce—all without result." All U.S. raid suspensions

evoked "only hostile actions" by Hanoi, Rusk said. "There is, therefore, no reason to believe that Hanoi is interested in proposals for mutual de-escalation such as those put forward by Sen. Kennedy."

Rusk Mar. 3 reiterated that U.S. bombing halts, similar to the one
proposed by Kennedy, had been tried without reciprocal action from
North Vietnam. Hanoi had insisted that a "permanent and unconditional" halt in U.S. air raids on North Vietnam remained one of its
conditions for peace talks, Rusk said. It was North Vietnam, Rusk insisted, not Soviet Premier Kosygin, that was the stumbling block to
peace.

Kennedy Mar. 4 disputed Rusk's contention that there was
nothing new in Kennedy's proposed peace plan. "This has not been
tried before because we have so far refused to accept the offer of
Kosygin and [North Vietnamese Premier] Pham Van Dong to go to
the negotiating table if we stopped the bombing," Kennedy said.
North Vietnam, Kennedy claimed, had changed its position by stating
that it would enter negotiations if the U.S. stopped the bombing. During his talks with British Prime Min. Wilson in London Feb. 6-13,
Kosygin had offered to help bring about peace talks, Kennedy said.
"That's a vitally important ingredient. I'm not saying let's do what
we've done before. The situation has changed dramatically. They [the
Communists] made the offer and I suggested we accept." Further
supporting his contention that his proposal was a new one, Kennedy
rejected the Administration's argument that the U.S. had carried out a
6-day raid halt during the *Tet* truce. Kennedy pointed out that the
first 4 days were part of the Feb. 8-12 general military cease-fire in
South Vietnam. The following 2-day raid suspension, Kennedy said,
had been requested by Britain and the Soviet Union during the
London talks and had not been volunteered by the U.S.

*Among other reactions to Kennedy's proposal to halt the bomb-
ing of North Vietnam:*

Mar.2—Sen. Henry Jackson: The adoption of Kennedy's proposal
would mean the U.S. "would get maneuvered into a position of weakness."...Sen. Mike Mansfield: Pres. Johnson, "by and large," had
done what Kennedy had proposed.

Mar.3—Sen. Charles Percy (R., Ill.): Kennedy's proposal was
useful in contrast to the Johnson Administration's peace overtures,
which were "simply too vague to be practical."...Sen. Everett M.
Dirksen (R., Ill.): "I can't see anything new" in Kennedy's proposal.
Johnson's refusal to halt the bombing without "equivalent action" by
the Communists to de-escalate their military activities was the proper
policy.... Rep. L. Mendel Rivers (D., S.C.): "You can bet your bot-
tom dollar" the U.S. would gain no advantage from unilaterally halting the bombing of North Vietnam.... Rep. Emanuel Celler (D.,
N.Y.): A U.S. halt in the raids on North Vietnam "would create pressures to intensify the war rather than encourage peace. In the past,

with every cessation of bombing, the hopes of our people for peace rose, only to be dashed by the negation of peace by the North Vietnamese."

Mar.5 —Richard M. Nixon: Kennedy's "proposals are not new....[They] have the effect of prolonging the war by encouraging the enemy. They are led to believe there is a division in the United States and they can win. Johnson is right and Kennedy is wrong."

Kennedy's proposals received strong support from such U.S. critics of the American bombing policy as Sens. J. William Fulbright (D., Ark.), Joseph S. Clark (D., Pa.) and John Sherman Cooper (R., Ky.).

The North Vietnamese Communist Party newspaper *Nhan Dan* said in an editorial Mar. 4 that Kennedy's speech and other "strong protests by public opinion" in the U.S. had put the U.S. government in an "awkward and embarrassing position." According to *Nhan Dan's* version of the speech: Kennedy had "denounced Johnson for 'steadily widening the war' and urged the U.S. Administration to halt bombing North Vietnam unconditionally so as to 'bring peace nearer'"; the Senator also had "urged the United States to recognize and talk with the South Vietnam National Liberation Front."

The Soviet government newspaper *Izvestia* conceded Mar. 4 that Kennedy had been "stressing his disagreement with the White House on the Vietnamese question" for a long time. But "one should not exaggerate the extent of this disagreement," the Soviet journal warned, because although Kennedy had called for a halt in the U.S. bombing of North Vietnam, he also "swore his solidarity with the purposes of American policy in Vietnam and prudently complimented the President for 'attempts to achieve an honorable peace.'"

Ho Rejects LBJ Proposal of Talks

The North Vietnamese press agency reported Mar. 21, 1967 that in a hitherto unpublicized exchange of notes with Pres. Johnson in February, Ho Chi Minh had rejected a proposal by Johnson for direct U.S.-North Vietnamese talks on ending the war. The U.S. State Department confirmed the exchange of letters and released them later Mar. 21. Johnson declared in a statement Mar. 21 that Ho's rejection of his suggestion was "a regrettable rebuff to a genuine effort to move toward peace." Johnson added: "This has been the consistent attitude of Hanoi to many efforts by us, by other governments, by groups of governments and by leading personalities. Nevertheless, we shall persevere in our efforts to find an honorable peace. Until that is achieved, we shall continue to do our duty in Vietnam."

Johnson's letter to Ho, dated Feb. 2 and delivered to a North Vietnamese representative in Moscow Feb. 8, said: "I am prepared to order a cessation of bombing against your country and the stopping of further augmentation of United States forces in Vietnam as soon as I am assured that infiltration into South Vietnam by land and by sea has stopped." This reciprocal de-escalation of military activities, the President said, would "make it possible for us to conduct serious and private discussions leading toward an early peace." In suggesting direct U.S.-North Vietnamese discussions, Johnson said that previous indirect messages between the 2 countries "may have been distorted or misinterpreted as they passed through these various channels." The President said that the talks could be held in Moscow, Burma or any other country.

Referring to the *Tet* truce, which later halted ground fighting in South Vietnam Feb. 8-12, Johnson told Ho that North Vietnam's proposal "would be greatly strengthened if your military authorities and those of . . . South Vietnam could promptly negotiate an extension" of the truce. The President said that the U.S. could not accept an unconditional and permanent halt in the bombing of North Vietnam and a cessation of other military activity as demanded by Hanoi. To do so, Johnson said, (1) "would inevitably produce worldwide speculation that discussions were under way and would impair the privacy and secrecy of those discussions" and (2) would raise U.S. government doubts about whether North Vietnam "would make use of such action by us to improve its military position."

Ho's reply, sent to Johnson Mar. 10 and received Mar. 15, reiterated the demands incorporated in North Vietnam's 4-point peace plan that the U.S. "must stop definitely and unconditionally its bombing raids and all other acts of war against" North Vietnam, "withdraw from South Vietnam all U.S. and satellite troops and let the Vietnamese people settle themselves their own affairs." North Vietnam would hold direct negotiations with the U.S. "only after the unconditional cessation of the U.S. bombing raids and all other acts of war against" North Vietnam, Ho said. He accused the U.S. of having "unleashed and intensified the war of aggression in South Vietnam with a view to prolonging the partition of Vietnam and turning South Vietnam into a neocolony and a military base of the United States." He said "broad sections of the American people" gave "strong sympathy and support" to the Viet Cong-North Vietnamese cause.

Kennedy Mar. 21 called Johnson's letter to Ho a stiffening of American conditions for ending the war. Kennedy said: Previously, Johnson and State Secy. Rusk had stated that the U.S. "require[d] a military de-escalation in return for a cessation of bombing"; Johnson's letter to Ho "adds to that the further condition that we have evidence that Hanoi has already ceased infiltration before we stop the bombing"; Johnson's letter "speaks of an unconditional and permanent end to the bombing as his interpretation of the North Vietnamese condition for negotiations," whereas Ho's answer "refers only to an unconditional halt in relation to negotiations and does not use the word 'permanent' in connection with the beginning of negotiations."

U.S. Administration officials asserted that Johnson's letter did not constitute a hardening of the American position. State Department spokesman Robert McCloskey said Johnson's letter had "re-affirmed earlier proposals made on 4 occasions by the U.S. government to Hanoi through representatives in Moscow, commencing in early June [1966]."

Johnson Policy Under Attack

An attack on Pres. Johnson's policy in Vietnam was mounted in the Senate Apr. 25, a day after U.S. jets bombed airbases in North Vietnam and the day after Gen. William Westmoreland, U.S. commander in Vietnam, had said that U.S. critics of the war fostered a belief by the enemy that "he can win politically" what he could not win "militarily." The major speech attacking Administration policy was delivered by Sen. George McGovern (D., S.D.). Sens. Kennedy, Fulbright, Frank Church (D., Ida.) and Ernest Gruening (D., Alaska) also joined in the attack. Sens. Spessard L. Holland (D., Fla.), Russell B. Long (D., La.) and Frank J. Lausche (D., O.) defended the Administration.

McGovern said: "In trying to imply that it is American dissent which is causing the Vietnamese to continue the war, the Administration is only confessing the weakness of its own case by trying to silence its critics and confuse the American people." "The new level of escalation marked by our bombing of the North Vietnamese airfields has brought us one step closer to World War III, involving the limitless legions of China backed by the enormous firepower of Soviet Russia."

After commending McGovern for his speech, Kennedy warned against the inevitability of escalation: "Is it not really inevitable that after the events of last week our adversaries in that part of the world will have to take other steps themselves?... The Soviet Union, Communist China and North Vietnam will have to react to what we have done by acting themselves.... We are certainly moving toward a serious escalation, and it is clear from the events of the past weeks that that is going to continue from our side and our adversaries." Kennedy opposed a policy of trying "to bring about a peace through military action, which is really going to bring about destruction of Vietnam and the people."

(Despite the Congressional attacks on U.S. policy in Vietnam, the Johnson Administration had little difficulty in winning Congressional approval of measures to pay for that policy. A bill appropriating $12,196,000 to finance the U.S. military effort in Vietnam through June 30 had been passed by 77-3 Senate vote Mar. 20 and House voice vote Mar. 21. It was signed by Pres. Johnson Apr. 4. The 3 Senate votes against the bill were cast by Sens. Gruening, Wayne Morse and Gaylord Nelson. Kennedy voted for the appropriation.)

The escalation of fighting in Vietnam also brought a more vociferous tone and more militant character to the protests mounted in the spring of 1967 by the anti-war movement in the U.S. Kennedy was reported Apr. 9 to have said in a University of Michigan newspaper interview that even though the war protesters were in the minority, their demonstrations were curbing Johnson's handling of the Vietnam conflict. The student newspaper, the *Michigan Daily,* quoted Kennedy as saying that the Administration "has been paying more attention to students and young people since the protests began." Kennedy said Americans were more aware "of what our national policy is because of the protests." He said he supported the minority view "that the bombs must be stopped."

16 Senate critics of Administration policy on Vietnam, including Kennedy, warned Hanoi in a statement issued May 17 that dissent on the war was a minority view in the U.S. and that "there are many more who either give their full endorsement to our government's policy in Vietnam, or who press for even greater military action there." The statement said that while the 16 Senators would press for "a negotiated peace," they "remain steadfastly opposed to any unilateral withdrawal of American troops from South Vietnam." A negotiated peace, they said, was "the last and only remaining alternative to a prolonged and intensified war." The statement originated with Sen. Frank Church, who had cleared it with State Secy. Rusk. Support for the statement was expressed May 17 by Vice Pres. Hubert H. Humphrey.

South Vietnamese Elections

The major development in the domestic affairs of war-torn South Vietnam during 1967 was the September election victory of Chief of State Nguyen Van Thieu, 44, as president of the republic and of Premier Nguyen Cao Ky, 37, as vice president. The elections, held under a new constitution, were seen as a test of the nation's progress toward responsible government. Semi-official American election observers reported that South Vietnam had met this test; opposition candidates and some American newsmen contradicted this view. Similar differences of opinion surrounded elections for the Senate (Sept. 3) and the House of Representatives (Oct. 22). Candidates who were openly neutralist or allegedly pro-Communist were not permitted to run.

Robert Kennedy had charged in the Senate Aug. 11, during the election campaign, that South Vietnam's ruling military junta was "making the election a fraud and a farce." "If there is no free election, if somebody asks 'what are you doing in South Vietnam?' what can one possibly argue?" he asked. "Without self-determination," he declared, "the rulers of South Vietnam will have denied their people the very rights for which more than 12,000 Americans have died." Kennedy said the issue arose "at a time when the military efforts of the South Vietnamese government have lessened and our own involvement has deepened. Over a recent 6-month period, our casualties were higher than South Vietnam's draft calls." Kennedy, however, reiterated his support of "the commitment of the U.S. in Vietnam" and said he did "not believe the U.S. should pull out unilaterally."

Kennedy said Sept. 4 that he hoped the election would result in the "opening of meaningful negotiations" with North Vietnam and the National Liberation Front. "Continuation of the extraordinarily large United States investment in Vietnam in men and money must be conditioned on the fulfillment" of responsibilities by the newly elected South Vietnamese presidential ticket, he said. The responsibilities included a "start of genuine land reform, an end to virtually unrestrained corruption and a substantial improvement in the economic life of the villages."

RFK Attacks Morality of U.S. Actions

Speaking Nov. 18 at Marymount College, a Catholic girls' school in Tarrytown, N.Y., Sen. Kennedy assailed the bombings of North Vietnam as immoral. During his talk he polled the students and their teachers and found that the majority favored more—not less—bombing. "Do you understand what that means, when you ask for more bombing?" he implored. "It means you are voting to send people, Americans and Vietnamese, to die.... Don't you understand that what we are doing to the Vietnamese is not very different than what Hitler did to the Jews?"

Kennedy said in the Nov. 18 talk that he had "no plans" to make a Presidential or Vice Presidential bid in 1968 and would support his party's nominees, specifically "the President and Mr. Humphrey if they are the nominees." As for the possible Presidential candidacy of Sen. Eugene J. McCarthy (D., Minn.), who was becoming widely known as one of the leading opponents of U.S. policy in Vietnam, Kennedy said this "would add a great deal of excitement and interest" and would allow Americans to "take out their frustration [over the war] in talk instead of violence."

McCarthy announced Nov. 30 that he would enter 5 or 6 Democratic Presidential primaries in 1968 to further the campaign for negotiated settlement of the war. If that effort did not bring about a policy change in this direction by the Johnson Administration, he warned, "I think this challenge would have to go all the way to a challenge for the nomination for the Presidency." "I am concerned," McCarthy declared at a crowded news conference in Washington, "that the Administration seems to have set no limit to the price which it's willing to pay for a military victory." McCarthy said that if his challenge went as far as an attempt at the nomination: "It may not be me at that point. It might be someone else, but so far as the end result of the effort, I think it has to go to the point of trying to change the policy and direction and also the mood of America with reference to the political problems of 1968." He had discussed this with Kennedy and Kennedy had not attempted to dissuade him and had made "no commitment to stand aside all the way," McCarthy said. McCarthy added that he would have been "glad" if Kennedy "had moved early," and if he had, "there'd have been no need for me to do anything." He was "hopeful" that his effort "may alleviate" somewhat "this sense of political helplessness and restore to many people a belief in the processes of American politics. . . ."

Gen. William C. Westmoreland, commander of U.S. forces in South Vietnam, and U.S. Amb.-to-South Vietnam Ellsworth Bunker had made a joint appearance Nov. 19 on the NBC-TV program "Meet the Press." Westmoreland claimed that U.S. and South Vietnamese troops were "winning a war of attrition." It was "conceivable that within 2 years or less the enemy will be so weakened that the Vietnamese will be able to cope with a greater share of the war burden," he declared. "We will be able to phase down the level of our military effort, withdraw some troops. . . ."

Westmoreland's view was disputed by Kennedy during a Nov. 26 appearance on the CBS-TV program "Face the Nation." "We are not going to win unless the South Vietnamese begin to do more, make more of an effort," Kennedy said.

During the Nov. 26 interview, Kennedy claimed that America's "moral position" in Vietnam had been undermined by the Johnson Administration. Prior to Pres. Johnson, Kennedy claimed, the U.S. was working to give the South Vietnamese the "right to decide their own future" so they "could select their own form of government." Currently, however, the U.S. was saying that it was fighting in South Vietnam "so we don't have to fight [the Communists] in Thailand, so that we don't have to fight on the West Coast of the United States." Previously the U.S. was helping the South Vietnamese, Kennedy continued. "Now we've changed and we've switched. Maybe they don't want it but we want it, so we're going in there and we're killing South Vietnamese, we're killing children, we're killing women, we're killing innocent people, because we don't want to have the war fought on American soil, or because they're 12,000 miles away and they might get to be 11,000 miles away. Our whole moral position changes, it seems to me, tremendously. Do we have the right here in the United States to say that we're going to kill 10s of thousands, make millions of people, as we have, refugees, kill women and children, as we have? There are 35,000 people without limbs in South Vietnam. There are 150,000 civilian casualties every year, thousands of children are killed because of our efforts. Do we have that right here in the United States to perform these acts because we want to protect ourselves? . . . I very seriously question whether we have that right.... Other people are carrying the burden. But this is also our war. Those of us who stay here in the United States, we must feel it when we use napalm, when a village is destroyed and civilians are killed. This is also our responsibility. This is a moral obligation and a moral responsibility for us here in the United States. And I think we have forgotten about that. And when we switched from one point of view to another, I think we have forgotten about that. And I think that it should be discussed and all of us should examine our own conscience on what we are doing in South Vietnam. It is not just the fact that we are killing North Vietnamese soldiers or Viet Cong; we are also responsible for 10s and 10s of thousands of innocent civilian casualties, and I think we are going to have a difficult time explaining this to ourselves."

During this Nov. 26 telecast Kennedy was asked whether he thought it would take a new President to negotiate a settlement in Vietnam. He replied "No. I think that Pres. Johnson could negotiate a settlement. I happen to disagree with the way we are going about it, but I think it could be done."

The question of whether or not Kennedy planned to enter the Presidential election race in competition to Lyndon B. Johnson came up 2 months later—in a context that apparently did not involve the dispute over Vietnamese war policy. The incident did not clarify Kennedy's intentions.

Kennedy conducted an off-the-record briefing for political reporters at the National Press Club Jan. 30, 1968. During the briefing Kennedy indicated that he would not seek the Democratic Presidential nomination and that he would support whomever the party nominated at the August convention in Chicago. At the end of the meeting it was agreed that the reporters could write that Kennedy had said that he had no plans to oppose Pres. Johnson "under any conceivable circumstances." Jules Witcover, one of the reporters present, reported in his book *85 Days: The Last Campaign of Robert Kennedy,* that Kennedy's press secretary, Frank Mankiewicz, then changed the quotation to "under any *foreseeable circumstances,*" phraseology that obviously did not preclude the possibility of Kennedy's entering the race. Kennedy offered no objections to the change.

North Vietnamese Foreign Min. Nguyen Duy Trinh had said Dec. 29, 1967 (in a statement broadcast by Hanoi radio Jan. 1, 1968) that his government would start talks if the U.S. unconditionally halted attacks against North Vietnam. His declaration stirred international speculation that Hanoi might have eased its conditions for peace negotiations. Heretofore, North Vietnam had insisted that talks could, rather than "will," be held after the U.S. ended hostilities. Many opponents of the Johnson Administration policy insisted that Trinh's statement constituted a clear offer of peace negotiations to the U.S.

Speaking in San Francisco Jan. 4, 1968 Kennedy suggested that the U.S. should respond to this apparent Hanoi offer: "It makes sense to go to the table and try to resolve the conflict. If we wait another year it will be far worse." Appearing with Sen. Gale McGee (D., Wyo.) Jan. 21 on a special CBS-TV program on Vietnam, Kennedy said the U.S. was "asking for unconditional surrender" as its terms for talks. Instead, he said, the bombing should be halted as an inducement to begin negotiations. McGee, who opposed a bombing halt, said it would be "totally irresponsible" to "go to any conference table strictly on a fishing expedition."

Kennedy Intensifies Attack on Johnson Policy

In a Chicago speech Feb. 8, Kennedy laid down his most vigorous challenge to date against Administration policies in Vietnam. Kennedy's speech was delivered one week after the Viet Cong and North Vietnamese had launched their most effective offensive of the war during the *Tet* holidays. The attacks, which were centered on South Vietnam's major cities, took the lives of almost 600 U.S. servicemen during the first week of stepped-up fighting.

Asserting that it was time "to take a new look at the war in Vietnam" and that "our nation must be told the truth," Kennedy said: "A total military victory is not within sight" and "probably beyond our grasp." It was an "illusion" to believe that "unswerving pursuit of military victory ... is in the interest of either ourselves or the people of Vietnam." Neither could the war remove the threat of communism in Asia, because "the outcome" of that issue depended in each country "on the intrinsic strength of the government, the particular circumstances of the country and the particular character of the insurgent movement." "We can and should offer reasonable assistance to Asia, but we cannot build a Great Society there if we cannot build one in our own country." "We must actively seek a peaceful settlement" in Vietnam and "can no longer harden our terms every time Hanoi indicates it may be prepared to negotiate, and we must be willing to foresee a settlement which will give the Viet Cong a chance to participate in the political life of the country." "A political compromise is not just the best path to peace but the only path, and we must show as much willingness to risk some of our prestige for peace as to risk the lives of young men in war." "We have misconceived the nature of the war" and "sought to resolve by military might a conflict whose issue depends upon the will and conviction of the South Vietnamese people." It was an "illusion that we can win a war which the South Vietnamese cannot win for themselves."

Kennedy also said: It was an "illusion" to think that "the American national interest is identical with—or should be subordinated to—the selfish interest of an incompetent military regime."

The current Saigon government was "unwilling or incapable of being an effective ally in the war against the Communists." The recent enemy offensive against the cities, "savagely striking at will across all of South Vietnam, has finally shattered the mask of official illusion with which we have concealed our true circumstances" and "demonstrated that no part or person of South Vietnam is secure from... attacks." A belief that the war could "be settled in our own way and in our own time on our own terms" was a still further "illusion." "Such a settlement is the privilege of... those who crush their enemies... or wear away their will to fight. We have not done this, nor is there any prospect we will." "The central battle in this war cannot be measured by body counts or bomb damage, but by the extent to which the people of South Vietnam act on a sense of common purpose and hope with those that govern them." "The best way to save our most precious stake in Vietnam—the lives of our soldiers—is to stop the enlargement of the war, and... the best way to end casualties is to end the war."

By all accounts Kennedy's Feb. 8 Chicago speech was his most devastating attack so far on Administration Vietnam policies. Jack Newfield, in his book *Robert Kennedy: A Memoir,* described it as "Kennedy's first Vietnam text that was not defensive, apologetic, and understated." The speech was made at the Book & Author luncheon of the Chicago *Sun-Times.* Kennedy had been invited to speak following the publication of his latest book, *To Seek a Newer World.* The book was essentially a compilation of Kennedy's previous statements and speeches on a variety of issues, foreign and domestic. In a newly prepared postscript to the book, Kennedy said: The "world's hope" was "to rely on youth." "It is a revolutionary world we live in; and this generation, at home and around the world, has had thrust upon it a greater burden of responsibility than any generation that has ever lived." Youth, however, must avoid 4 dangers: (1) "The danger of futility, the belief that there is nothing one man or woman can do against the enormous array of the world's ills." (2) "Expediency"—"Rejection of those who say that hopes and beliefs must bend before immediate necessities." (3) "Timidity"—"Few men are willing to brave the disapproval of their fellows, the censure of their colleagues, the wrath of their society." (4) "Comfort"—"The temptation to follow the easy and familiar paths of personal ambition and financial success so grandly spread before those who enjoy the privilege of education."

With the exception of the last item, these, ironically, were the character defects that many of the nation's youth attributed to Kennedy because of his delay in opposing the war and in entering the Democratic race for President.

In his book Kennedy spoke out forcefully against a unilateral U.S. withdrawal from South Vietnam: "Withdrawal is now impossible. Those people [the South Vietnamese allied with the U.S.]

cannot suddenly be abandoned to the forcible conquest of a minority...." "I believe defeat or precipitous withdrawal from Vietnam [would] damage our position in the world. We would not suddenly collapse; Communist fleets would not suddenly appear in the harbors of Honolulu or San Francisco Bay. But there would be serious effects, especially in Southeast Asia itself."

Kennedy urged Mar. 7 that the Johnson Administration consult the Senate prior to any further escalation of the U.S. effort in Vietnam. Speaking in the Senate, Kennedy said: For the past 7 years—during both the Kennedy and Johnson Administrations—the U.S. had invariably escalated whenever it faced difficulties in Vietnam. When this was done, U.S. spokesmen always insisted "that victory is just ahead of us. The fact is that victory is not just ahead of us. It was not in 1961 or 1962, when I was one of those who predicted there was a light at the end of the tunnel. There was not in 1963 or 1964 or 1965 or 1966 or 1967, and there is not now."

In his Mar. 7 speech, Kennedy denounced what he described as the immorality of U.S. policies: "Are we like the God of the Old Testament that can decide, in Washington, D.C., what cities, what towns, what hamlets in Vietnam are going to be destroyed? Is it because we think it may possibly protect the people of Thailand, the people of Malaysia, the people of Hawaii, or keep certain people out of Texas or California or Massachusetts or New York? Or do we have that authority to kill 10s and 10s of thousands of people because we say we have a commitment to the South Vietnamese people? But have they been consulted...? Do we have the authority to put hundreds of thousands of people—in fact, millions of people—into refugee camps or should these decisions be left to them?"

In what was becoming one of his major complaints about the war, Kennedy criticized the South Vietnamese for not undertaking a greater share of the fighting. "If we are going to draft American troops of 18 and 19 years of age" and send them to Vietnam, "are we also going to say—as we now are doing—that the people of South Vietnam do not have to draft their own 18-year-old and 19-year-old boys?" Kennedy also said in his Mar. 7 speech:

"I rise to join the Senator from Arkansas [J.W. Fulbright] in urging that before any further major step is taken in connection with the war in Vietnam, the Senate be consulted. No issue... has so divided the United States, in many, many years, as has the war in Vietnam.... It seems to me that if we are going to take this step in connection with the war in Vietnam, it would be well to take whatever steps are possible to get concurrence and support of the Senate, and of the American people. I think it would be a mistake for the executive branch and for the President to take a step toward escalation of the conflict in the next several weeks without having the support and understanding of the Senate, and of the American people...."

"It seems to me if we have learned anything over the period of the last 7 years, it is the fact that just continuing to send more troops, or increasing the bombing, is not the answer in Vietnam. We have tried that. It seems to me something different should be tried....

"As to our own interests in Vietnam, could not the Germans or the Russians have argued the same thing before the beginning of World War II—that they had the right to go into Poland, into Estonia, into Latvia, into Lithuania, because they needed them for their own protection, that they needed them as a buffer? I question whether we have that right in this country.

"It seems to me before we take major steps, to send perhaps 200,000 more troops to Vietnam, that we should ask some very, very significant questions. I would like to know what the purpose would be of sending more American troops there, and what they could accomplish that has not been accomplished by the American troops that are already there. I would like to know what the people of South Vietnam are going to be willing to do themselves....

"When our own Marines are going into Hue to recapture it, do we have the right to stand by and merely look at thousands of South Vietnamese looting Hue that has been liberated by us? Do we have to accept that? Do we have to accept the situation in which we are told that a young man in South Vietnam is running his father's factory because he paid off his draft board and does not have to go? When this was brought to the attention of the President, he replied that there is stealing in Beaumont, Tex. If there is stealing in Beaumont, Tex., it is not bringing about the death of American boys. Officials have said, as reported this afternoon, that there is deepseated corruption in South Vietnam. Do we have to accept that? Who is our commitment to? Is it to Ky, or to Thieu?...

"I know some have said that we should intensify the bombing in the North. They should be heard. I do not happen to believe that is the answer to the problem, but I do know that what we have been doing is not the answer, that it is not suitable, that it is immoral and intolerable to continue it.

"If we are going to continue what we have been doing, when we were told we were just a little way from victory before, and send 100,000 men or 200,000 more men there, the Senate should be consulted and its approval should be received."

QUEST FOR THE PRESIDENCY

RFK Announces Candidacy

Robert Kennedy Mar. 16, 1968 announced his candidacy for the Democratic Presidential nomination. His candidacy was presumed to be in opposition to Pres. Johnson, who, it was assumed, planned to seek renomination. Kennedy's announcement followed by 4 days what most observers considered a victory by Sen. Eugene McCarthy in the New Hampshire Democratic primary. McCarthy nearly defeated Johnson in the popular vote and won a majority of the state's delegates to the national Democratic convention.

McCarthy, the only major Democrat on the ballot, won about 42% of the vote in his surprising show of strength against the President, who polled 49% on a write-in vote. An organized write-in campaign for Johnson had been supported by the Democratic state committee and led by Gov. John W. King, Sen. Thomas J. McIntyre and Bernard Boutin, former Small Business Administrator. McCarthy had campaigned actively in the state as a critic of Johnson's Vietnam policy. He won 20 Democratic national convention delegate votes; Johnson won only 4.

Jack Newfield reported in *Robert Kennedy: A Memoir* that Kennedy had decided to run Mar. 5, a week before the New Hampshire primary. Newfield wrote that Robert Kennedy then instructed his brother, Edward (Ted), to inform McCarthy that he was "probably" going to enter the race after the Wisconsin primary Apr. 2. Ted Kennedy, according to Newfield, did not relay that message to McCarthy out of fear that McCarthy would use it against the Kennedys. Robert Kennedy flew to Washington from New York Mar. 13, the day after the New Hampshire primary. On landing at Washington's National Airport, Kennedy told reporters he was "reassessing the possibility of whether I will run against Pres. Johnson" for the Democratic Presidential nomination. According to Newfield: "The last week of the secret discussions about how best to enter the race were suddenly obsolete. Kennedy did not explain that he had been tortured by ambivalence for 6 months, or that he had virtually decided to run 8 days earlier. In a few careless seconds he resurrected the sleeping stereotype of himself as a ruthless opportunist."

Walter Cronkite asked Kennedy that afternoon to appear that evening on his CBS-TV news broadcast. Kennedy agreed and, in the Cronkite interview, acknowledged that he was considering entering the race against Pres. Johnson. McCarthy's victory in New Hampshire was important in that regard, he said. Before then, "I was reluctant to become involved in this struggle because I thought it might turn into a personal conflict between Pres. Johnson and myself and that the issues that I believe strongly in and which I think are being ignored at the moment would be passed over." New Hampshire, however, "has demonstrated that there is a deep division within the Democratic Party," he continued. "One of the major reasons that I didn't want to become involved earlier was because I thought that I might be the instrument of dividing the country in a way that would be difficult to put back together [or] dividing the Democratic Party in a very damaging way."

Kennedy announced his candidacy Mar. 16 at a news conference in the Caucus Room of the Senate Office Building, the same room in which John Kennedy had begun his campaign 8 years previously. Following his news conference, Kennedy left for New York and his first campaign appearance, at that city's St. Patrick's Day Parade. 80 days later Robert Kennedy's campaign ended with his murder in the pantryway of a Los Angeles hotel. During those 12 weeks that Kennedy was a Presidential candidate, Pres. Johnson announced that he would not seek reelection, Martin Luther King Jr. was assassinated, the Paris peace talks began and Vice Pres. Hubert Humphrey declared himself a candidate for the Democratic Presidential nomination.

Declaring his candidacy, Kennedy warned in his televised news conference Mar. 16 that he was "convinced that this country is on a perilous course." He said: "I run to seek new policies—policies to end the bloodshed in Vietnam and in our cities, policies to close the gap that now exists between black and white, between rich and poor, between young and old in this country and around the rest of the world ... I run because it is now unmistakably clear that we can change these disastrous, divisive policies only by changing the men who are now making them." "The reality of recent events in Vietnam has been glossed over with illusions...." In "private talks and in public I have tried in vain to alter our course in Vietnam before it further saps our spirit and our manpower, further raises the risk of wider war and further destroys the country and the people it was meant to save. I cannot stand aside from the contest that will decide our nation's future and our children's future."

In a question-and-answer session with reporters following the reading of his formal statement, Kennedy said: "Basically, I'm in favor of de-escalating the struggle there [in Vietnam]. I'm basically in favor of the South Vietnamese taking over more of the effort and less of the effort being in the hands of the United States government and American soldiers. I'm in favor of our making it quite clear to the South Vietnamese that their corruption should end, that they have to have a general mobilization and that they have to draft 18-year-olds and 19-year-olds, and I'm in favor of negotiating with the National Liberation Front as I have said, and I think that we have to make it clear that the National Liberation Front is going to play a role in the future political process of South Vietnam. And I've also said in the past that I think that ... the North Vietnamese have refused to come to the negotiating table until we have stopped the bombing. I'm in favor of taking that step. They have not requested or suggested that it be done on a permanent basis and, as I have said, if the negotiations are unsuccessful or if they use that period of time in a way that is adverse to our military forces there, then I think that we can take retaliatory action."

Kennedy declared Mar. 17 that he would have "grave reservations" about supporting Johnson if the Democrats renominated him and the Republicans nominated a candidate favoring de-escalation in Vietnam. Johnson's policies "could be catastrophic," he warned.

Kennedy Offer Not to Run Reported

Reports circulated Mar. 17, the day after Kennedy's announcement of candidacy, asserted that he would have agreed to stay out of the Presidential race had Pres. Johnson agreed to appoint a top-level commission to study a shift in U.S. policy in Vietnam. Kennedy and his aides immediately branded the story as a distortion circulated by the White House to discredit his candidacy. The initial reports of the incident were broadcast by Roger Mudd of CBS Mar. 17 and published Mar. 19 by both *Time* and *Newsweek* magazines.

According to the *Newsweek* version (issue dated March 25): Kennedy adviser Theodore Sorensen, a former aide to Presidents John Kennedy and Johnson, met secretly with Johnson at the White House Mar. 11 as "an honest broker" between Kennedy and the President. Sorensen promised that Kennedy would agree not to run if the President appointed a commission "to re-evaluate" the U.S. involvement in Vietnam. Johnson "expressed interest." Kennedy, his brother, Sen. Edward M. Kennedy, and Sorensen "pursued the proposal" at a secret meeting Mar. 14 with Defense Secy. Clark Clifford. Robert Kennedy suggested to Clifford a Presidential statement that the war "required re-evaluation" and a Presidential commission to do the study. He suggested as members himself and 9 others, persons "whose well-established views left no doubt that their recommendation would change the course of the war." Clifford took the proposal to Johnson, who objected because "it was a political deal," "provided encouragement for Hanoi" and "amounted to an abdication of Presidential authority." Clifford informed Sorensen later Mar. 14 of the rejection.

Kennedy Mar. 17 called reports of the incident an "incredible distortion" and suggested that the Administration had leaked the allegedly distorted reports contrary to "the traditional rules of confidence governing White House conversations." The affair was illustrative of why "the American people no longer believe the President," Kennedy declared. He said that he and Clifford had discussed the commission plan "not as a proposal by either of us" and that he had stressed that if the commission "were more than a public relations gimmick" and its creation and membership "signaled a clear-cut willingness to seek a wider path to peace in Vietnam," he would consider his candidacy unnecessary.

According to the Kennedy version: Sorensen's meeting with the President Mar. 11 was at Johnson's invitation. Sorensen broached the idea of a commission that could recommend a new Vietnam policy. But both Johnson and Kennedy had first heard the proposal from a Midwestern Democratic leader. (Reliable, subsequent reports identified this party leader as Chicago Mayor Richard Daley.) The President liked the idea, and the White House Mar. 13 asked for recommendations on membership from Sorensen, who had discussed the idea with Kennedy. Edward Kennedy then arranged for Robert Kennedy to meet Mar. 14 with Sorenson and Clifford. The idea for a commission was not, however, attributed to Robert Kennedy. At the Mar. 14 meeting Robert Kennedy said his "declaration of candidacy would no longer be necessary" if the plan were adopted; he would serve on the commission but did not insist on it and felt he should not be chairman. He and Sorensen suggested members for the commission. Clifford later informed Sorensen of the President's rejection of the proposal because (a) it would displease Senate committee chairmen if Kennedy were on the commission, (b) the President already knew of the views of its proposed members and could consult them, and (c) the idea was close to being a "political deal." Later, a White House aide, unaware of the plan's rejection, called Sorensen for his recommendations on names. Later "that night" Kennedy "decided to run for President."

Sorensen said Mar. 23 that his meeting with Johnson was at the President's invitation and "not related in the slightest" to Kennedy's decision to become a Presidential candidate. He said he "was not representing" Kennedy at the meeting and "did not clear the commission proposal" with Kennedy.

Sen. Eugene McCarthy Mar. 18 called Kennedy's offer on the commission "untenable" and "offensive to the Senate Foreign Relations Committee," the constitutionally-based source of advice to the President.

Kennedy Opens Campaign, Assails Johnson

Kennedy's Presidential campaign began Mar. 18. He made it apparent during his first campaign tour Mar. 18-25 that he intended to wage a campaign of vigorous criticism of Pres. Johnson's policies. Speaking before a wildly cheering audience at Kansas State University in Manhattan, Kan. Mar. 18, Kennedy denounced Johnson's Vietnam policy as "bankrupt." He assailed corruption in

South Vietnam and the South Vietnamese practice of buying deferments from military service "while American Marines die at Khesanh." "I ask for your help," he told the crowd. "If you will give me your help, if you will give me your hand, I will work for you and we will have a new America." "There is a contest on, not for the rule of America, but for the heart of America," he continued. "In these next 8 months, we are going to decide what the country will stand for and what kind of men we are."

Although he criticized the Saigon regime, Kennedy also assailed the "brutal" Viet Cong. "They have shown their willingness to sacrifice innocent civilians, to engage in torture and murder and despicable terror to achieve their ends," Kennedy said. There can be "no easy moral answer to this war, no one-sided condemnation of American actions. What we must ask ourselves is whether we have a right to bring so much destruction to another land."

Kennedy had begun his Kansas State speech with a quip about Johnson's rejection of the proposed Vietnam commission. "Really the only difference between us is that I wanted Sen. Mansfield, Sen. Fulbright and Sen. Morse appointed to the commission," Kennedy told the students, "and Pres. Johnson in his own inimitable style wanted to appoint Gen. Westmoreland, John Wayne and Martha Raye." Kennedy then quoted with approval this statement, which he attributed to William Allen White, the late editor of the *Emporia Gazette:* "If our colleges and universities do not breed men who riot, who rebel, who attack life with all the youthful vigor, then there is something wrong with our colleges. The more riots that come on college campuses, the better world for tomorrow."

Among Kennedy's remarks concerning Vietnam:

"I do not want—as I believe most Americans do not want—to sell out American interests, to simply withdraw, to raise the white flag of surrender. That would be unacceptable to us as a country and as a people. But I am concerned—as I believe most Americans are concerned—that the course we are following at the present time is deeply wrong. I am concerned—as I believe most Americans are concerned—that we are acting as if no other nations existed, against the judgment and desires of neutrals and our historic allies alike. I am concerned—as I believe most Americans are concerned—that our present course will not bring victory; will not bring peace; will not stop the bloodshed; and will not advance the interests of the United States or the cause of peace in the world. I am concerned that, at the end of it all, there will only be more Americans killed; more of our treasure spilled out; and because of the bitterness and hatred on every side of this war, more hundreds of thousands of Vietnamese slaughtered; so that they may say, as Tacitus said of Rome: 'They made a desert, and called it peace.'"

"I was involved in many of the early decisions on Vietnam, decisions which helped set us on our present path. It may be that the effort was doomed from the start; that it was never really possible to bring all the people of South Vietnam under the rule of the successive governments we supported—governments, one after another, riddled with corruption, inefficiency and greed; governments which did not and could not successfully capture and energize the national feeling of their people. If that is the case, as it well may be, then I am willing to bear my share of the responsibility, before history and before my fellow-citizens. But past error is no excuse for its own perpetuation. Tragedy is a tool for the living to gain wisdom, not a guide by which to live. Now as ever, we do ourselves best justice when we measure ourselves against ancient tests, as in the Antigone of Sophocles: 'All men make mistakes, but a good man yields when he knows his course is wrong, and repairs the evil. The only sin is pride.' "

"An American commander said of the town of Bentre, 'It became necessary to destroy the town in order to save it.' It is difficult to quarrel with the decision of American commanders to use air power and artillery to save the lives of their men. If American troops are to fight for Vietnamese cities, they deserve protection. What I cannot understand is why the responsibility for the recapture and attendant destruction of Hue and Bentre and the others should fall to American troops in the first place. If Communist insurgents or invaders held New York or Washington or San Francisco, we would not leave it to foreigners to take them back, and destroy them and their people in the process. Rather I believe there is not one among us who would not tear the invaders out with his bare hands, whatever the cost. There is no question that some of the South Vietnamese army fought with great bravery. The Vietnamese—as these units and the Viet Cong have both shown us—are a courageous people. But it is also true that a thousand South Vietnamese soldiers, in Hue on leave for *Tet,* hid among the refugees for 3 weeks, making no attempt to rejoin their units or join the town's defense; among them was a full colonel. And it is also true that in the height of the battle for Hue, as trucks brought back American dead and wounded from the front lines, millions of Americans could see, on their television screens, South Vietnamese soldiers occupied in looting the city those Americans were fighting to recapture."

"We can—as I have urged for 2 years, but as we have never done—negotiate with the National Liberation Front. We can—as we have never done—assure the Front a genuine place in the political life of South Vietnam. We can—as we are refusing to do today—begin to de-escalate the war, concentrate on protecting populated areas, and thus save American lives and slow down the destruction of the countryside. We can—as we have never done—insist that the government of South Vietnam broaden its base, institute real reforms, and seek an honorable settlement with their fellow countrymen.

"This is no radical program of surrender. This is no sell-out of American interests. This is a modest and reasonable program, designed to advance the interests of this country and save something from the wreckage for the people of Vietnam."

The North Vietnamese government, in its first comments on Kennedy's candidacy, indicated Mar. 20 a coolness toward both Kennedy and Sen. Eugene McCarthy. Hanoi radio said: "What must be noted is that among the American politicians who are fiercely wrangling with one another, none voices his support for the Vietnamese people's right to self-determination or expresses sympathy for our people's struggle for national liberation. All their quarrels center on how to retrieve U.S. failure in Vietnam; whether or not to increase the troops and, if the troops are to be increased, whether by a large or small number; where to get more troops; where to get more money to spend for the war; whether to continue the military escalation or to withdraw to the enclaves, and whether to expand the war or to try to withdraw with honor."

Kennedy visited Georgia, Alabama and Tennessee Mar. 21, making stops in Atlanta, the University of Alabama in Tuscaloosa and Vanderbilt University in Nashville. Jules Witcover, a reporter who covered the Kennedy campaign, said in *85 Days: The Last Campaign of Robert Kennedy:* "He made certain at each stop to emphasize he was not advocating unilateral withdrawal from Vietnam."

At Vanderbilt, Kennedy said: "We know we do not want to surrender, to simply run up the white flag. But we also see the wreckage of confident predictions of victory and all the terrible costs of our present course—the millions of refugees, the mothers and children scarred by bombs and napalm, the utter devastation and degradation of war. We see all this, and we ask: Does this serve the national interest? In what way does the war's present course advance the security of this country, the welfare of Vietnam or the cause of peace in the world? We ask this, and say with Camus: 'I should like to be able to love my country and still love justice.' We know then that all this is our responsibility, yours and mine and millions like us, and that it is far too important a matter to be entrusted to remote generals and leaders. We sense that this is not what the American spirit is really about. So I dissent. And you dissent. And we are going to turn this course around."

Kennedy toured California Mar. 24 and 25. He spoke with emotion in criticizing the South Vietnamese for not doing a greater share of the fighting. At night he would say, "Here, while the moon shines, our brave young men are dying in the swamps of Vietnam." During the day he substituted the word "sun" and asked: Which of the American war dead "might have written a poem? Which of them might have played in a World Series or given us the gift of laughter from a stage or helped build a bridge or a university? Which of them would have taught a child to read? It is our responsibility to let these men live. And that is why I run for President of the United States."

At a rally in San Jose Mar. 24, Kennedy drew cheers when he said: "If we can ask our 18- and 19-year-olds to fight and die in Vietnam, we can ask the South Vietnamese to do the same damned thing." Young Americans who have not been sent to Vietnam have become alienated by Pres. Johnson's policies, he said. "We must bring them back into American life. That is why I am running for President and that is why I ask your help."

Kennedy, speaking at the Greek Theatre in Los Angeles the night of Mar. 24, accused the Johnson Administration of "calling upon the darker impulses of the American spirit—not, perhaps deliberately, but through its action and the example it sets—an example where integrity, truth, honor and all the rest seem like words to fill out speeches rather than guiding beliefs."

At about this point in the campaign several influential journalists were beginning to express alarm about the tone of Kennedy's campaign remarks, especially the "darker impulses" statement. Robert J. Donovan, Washington bureau chief of the *Los Angeles Times,* wrote Mar. 26 that the lesson of the Kennedy campaign to date "is that when a war becomes a flaming political issue, the line between debate and demagoguery becomes a thin one. A candidate can easily be carried across it in the ardor of the fight." *Washington Post* reporter Richard Harwood, describing Kennedy's Mar. 21 Southern swing, had said: "Sen. Robert Kennedy invaded the South today and accused Pres. Johnson of creating the worst divisions in America since the Civil War. Going further, he implied that the President is to blame for the alienation and drug addiction among American youth, for rebelliousness and draft resistance on American campuses and for the 'anarchists' and rioters in American cities."

Asked whether he approved of individuals refusing to be drafted, Kennedy said Mar. 25: "I think he [the man called] would have to face the consequences. If I were to be called up, I would go. Each person has to examine his own conscience and do what he thinks is right." Kennedy's comment was in response to a student's question at San Fernando Valley State College, Northridge, Calif. During his talk there, he criticized State Secy. Dean Rusk, who was said to have told reporters at an off-the-record briefing that criticism of the Administration's Vietnam policies had reached the point where it raised the question: "Whose side are you on?" Kennedy said: "I am on the side of those who are not afraid to recognize past error, who refuse to blindly pursue bankrupt policies which will rend us from our friends and drain us of our treasure, in the fruitless pursuit of illusions long since shattered. I'm on the side of those who do not shout down others but who listen, challenge and then propose a better policy for America."

Following his frenzied weekend in California, Kennedy spent a week campaigning in Oregon, Washington, Idaho, Colorado, Nebraska, New Mexico and Arizona.

Speaking at Portland University Mar. 26, Kennedy acknowledged that the South Vietnamese "have now announced that they are going to draft 18- and 19-year-olds." (South Vietnam's Pres. Nguyen Van Thieu had announced in February that his government would curtail draft deferments and draft youths at 18 and 19.) Kennedy told the Portland University students that he did not favor U.S. student draft deferments. "The burden must be carried equally by all elements of society," he said.

At the University of Nebraska in Lincoln Mar. 28, Kennedy asked his audience: "Can you think of any new course suggested by Richard Nixon in Vietnam other than to do more of what we are doing?"

At a fund-raising dinner in Phoenix, Ariz. Mar. 30 Kennedy said: "Everywhere [he campaigned] the first issue is the war in Vietnam," and the "vast majority of Americans want a negotiated peace." After 20,000 deaths and the expenditure of $50 billion, Americans were tired of "promises of victory just around the corner." "They want this war to be honorably settled at the conference table not in some indefinite future, but while something still remains of the country of Vietnam and our hopes for domestic progress." "The American people are deeply troubled by that war, by the constant predictions of victory, which somehow lead only to more escalation, more American troops, more American casualties. They are concerned about the military regime we are supporting in Vietnam—about the corruption and inefficiency and sloth which have led Americans to fight a war we knew the Vietnamese would have to win themselves. And the American people are deeply troubled by the cost of this war, the cost of all the sad destruction to the people of Vietnam. For the American people are not cruel and insensitive to the sufferings of others. This is a compassionate and generous nation."

Several times during his week-long western tour Kennedy asked for a show of hands from his audiences on 3 positions relating to the war. According to the *N.Y. Times,* the pattern was as follows: On unilateral withdrawal from Vietnam, only a few hands went up; on stepping up the military effort, a sprinkling of hands went up; on stopping the bombing of North Vietnam, negotiating with the National Liberation Front, and scaling down the ground war—Kennedy's position—the vast majority of hands went up.

Johnson Quits Race, Curbs Vietnam Bombing

Pres. Johnson surprised politicians and the public Mar. 31 by announcing that he would not run for renomination. Such a decision had not been raised even as a possibility in the nation's press. The announcement came at the end of an address to the nation televised by all 3 major networks.

Earlier in the speech Johnson announced that he had ordered—"unilaterally"—a halt to air and naval bombardment of North Vietnam "except in the area north of the demilitarized zone where the continuing enemy build-up directly threatens allied forward positions and where the movement of their troops and supplies are clearly related to that threat." "The area in which we are stopping our attacks includes almost 90% of North Vietnam's population and most of its territory," Johnson said. "Thus, there will be no attacks around the principal populated areas, or in the food-producing areas of North Vietnam." He asserted that "even this very limited bombing of the North could come to an early end—if our restraint is matched by restraint in Hanoi." The President called on North Vietnamese Pres. Ho Chi Minh "to respond positively and favorably to this new step toward peace."

The President's 40-minute address was devoted almost entirely to the subject of the war in Vietnam. In the speech he announced that he was sending 13,500 more U.S. troops to Vietnam. Some of them would be members of Reserve units he was ordering to duty. Further defense expenditures—$2.5 billion in fiscal 1968 and $2.6 billion in fiscal 1969—were also requested by the President to meet the costs of the troop build-ups and military supplies since the beginning of the year and the cost of re-equipping the South Vietnamese forces and of meeting "our responsibilities in Korea."

The U.S. and North Vietnam agreed Apr. 3 to establish direct contact between their representatives as a first step toward ending the fighting in Vietnam. In response to Johnson's speech, the North Vietnamese government Apr. 3 "declared its readiness" to arrange for a meeting with a U.S. representative "with a view to determining...the unconditional cessation of the U.S. bombing raids and all other acts of war against the Democratic Republic of Vietnam so that talks may start."

At a news conference in New York Apr. 1, Kennedy had praised the President's decision. Kennedy said he had sent the President a telegram "respectfully and earnestly" requesting a personal meeting to discuss "how we might work together in the interest of national unity during the coming months" and expressing his "fervent...hope that your new efforts toward peace in Vietnam will succeed." "Your decision regarding the Presidency subordinates self to country and is truly magnanimous," Kennedy said in the telegram.

In a prepared statement at his Apr. 1 press conference, Kennedy said: Americans "want peace in Vietnam produced not by surrender of either side but by a negotiated settlement that realistically takes into account as quickly as possible the need for all Vietnamese and only Vietnamese to determine the future of their own country. I've long urged that we make the first step in this direction by a de-escalation of our military effort, halting the bombings of the North, insisting upon reforms in the South and pressing for negotiations with all parties looking toward a transfer of the present conflict from the military to the political arena. I am hopeful that the actions announced by the President will prove to be a step toward peace. It is obviously a critical time and I think it would be inappropriate to offer any detailed comment regarding those actions at this time."

In the question-and-answer period that followed the reading of his prepared statement, Kennedy was asked what his reaction would be if the North Vietnamese increased their military activity during the bombing cutback. He replied: "I've answered that question at various times before. And, as I said in my statement, I think it's not— could not serve a useful purpose at this time in view of the President's statement last night to go into any details in those matters."

Kennedy toured the Philadelphia-Camden area Apr. 1 and 2. At an outdoor rally in Camden, N.J. Apr. 1, he said: "We take pride in Pres. Johnson, who brought to final fulfillment the [New Deal] policies of 30 years and who yesterday sacrificed personal political considerations to win the peace for which all Americans yearn... The peace is above all what they want for the future. They will respect and honor Pres. Johnson, who has sought to take the first step toward peace."

Speaking at the University of Pennsylvania in Philadelphia Apr. 2, however, Kennedy again criticized Johnson's Vietnam policies. Kennedy said: "I think we have to reexamine our whole position in Vietnam.... We have to remind ourselves that the war is not over, the bombs are still falling 200 miles north of the demilitarized zone and reservists are still being called up. Stopping the bombing must be part of a coordinated plan" to attain a negotiated peace. "The first thing we must recognize is that we will have to negotiate with the National Liberation Front. It is silly for our government to act as if the NLF does not exist. They are not going to come in just to surrender and give their swords as we did at Appomattox and be given back their horses and told to go home for the spring plowing."

(Kennedy spoke that night at a Democratic fund-raising dinner in Philadelphia, and he called Philadelphia's mayor, James Tate, an avowed hawk, "one of the greatest mayors in the U.S.")

King's Murder Halts Campaign

Campaigning for the Presidential nominations was recessed by the candidates the night of Apr. 4 as they learned of the murder of the Rev. Dr. Martin Luther King Jr. in Memphis, Tenn. earlier that evening.

Kennedy had been scheduled to speak at an outdoor rally in a poor, black section of Indianapolis the night the Negro leader was slain. When he arrived at the rally, Kennedy found that the crowd of about 1,000 persons had not learned of King's assassination. He therefore announced: "I have bad news for you, for all of our fellow citizens and people who love justice all over the world, and that is that Martin Luther King was shot and killed tonight."

Kennedy, speaking without notes, said:

"Martin Luther King dedicated his life to love and to justice for his fellow human beings, and he died because of that effort. In this difficult day, in this difficult time for the United States, it is perhaps well to ask what kind of a nation we are and what direction we want to move in.

"For those of you who are black—considering the evidence there evidently is that there were white people who were responsible—you can be filled with bitterness, with hatred and a desire for revenge. We can move in that direction as a country, in great polarization—black people amongst black, white people amongst white, filled with hatred toward one another. Or we can make an effort, as Martin Luther King did, to understand and to comprehend, and to replace that violence, that stain of bloodshed that has spread across our land with an effort to understand with compassion and love.

"For those of you who are black and are tempted to be filled with hatred and distrust, at the injustice of such an act, against all white people, I can only say that I feel in my own heart the same kind of feeling. I had a member of my family killed, but he was killed by a white man. But we have to make an effort in the United States, we have to make an effort to understand, to go beyond these rather difficult times. My favorite poet was Aeschylus. He wrote: 'In our sleep, pain which cannot forget falls drop by drop upon the heart until, in our own despair, against our will, comes wisdom through the awful grace of God.'

"What we need in the United States is not division; what we need in the United States is not hatred; what we need in the United States is not violence or lawlessness, but love and wisdom, and compassion toward one another, and a feeling of justice toward those who still suffer within our country, whether they be white or they be black.

"So I shall ask you tonight to return home, to say a prayer for the family of Martin Luther King, that's true, but more importantly to say a prayer for our own country, which all of us love—a prayer for understanding and that compassion of which I spoke.

"We can do well in this country. We will have difficult times. We've had difficult times in the past. We will have difficult times in the future. It is not the end of violence; it is not the end of lawlessness; it is not the end of disorder. But the vast majority of white people and the vast majority of black people in this country want to live together, want to improve the quality of our life, and want justice for all human beings who abide in our land.

"Let us dedicate ourselves to what the Greeks wrote so many years ago: to tame the savageness of man and to make gentle the life of this world. Let us dedicate ourselves to that and say a prayer for our country and for our people."

Campaign Resumed

Kennedy resumed his campaign Apr. 10 following King's funeral in Atlanta Apr. 9. He toured mainly in the key primary states of Indiana, Nebraska, Oregon and California, where he campaigned against Sen. McCarthy. Vice Pres. Hubert H. Humphrey Apr. 27 announced his candidacy for the Democratic nomination for President. Humphrey declared his candidacy too late for him to enter any of the primary races.

With Pres. Johnson out of the race and with peace talks with the North Vietnamese set to begin, the war became an almost subordinate issue for most of the remainder of the Kennedy campaign. Although Kennedy continued to discuss the war, his major theme became the need for racial justice and reconciliation in the U.S. In Indiana he emphasized his having been U.S. Attorney General—the "chief law enforcement officer of the country." He spoke of the need to curb "lawlessness and violence in the streets" and of the desirability substituting jobs for "welfare handouts."

In Lansing, Mich. Apr. 11 Kennedy called for an intensive effort to end the war, to return "the major burden of the war to the South Vietnamese—where it should have been all along—and [to] lessen...the cost in American lives and money for as long as the fighting on the ground continues."

In Charleston, W. Va. Apr. 13, Kennedy said: "We must learn, whether in Southeast Europe or Southeast Asia, to deal with nations not as a monolithic Communist movement, which no longer exists, not as tools of far-away capitals, which cannot control them, but as nations whose significance and possible danger to our own national security must be carefully weighed on a case-by-case basis."

In Portland, Ore. Apr. 17, in a speech before the Sigma Delta Chi journalism fraternity, Kennedy said that "there is no task more important for this country, for this administration and for the next President of the United States than to end the war in Vietnam—to end it honorably, without surrender of our limited interests." McCarthy challenged Kennedy that day to debate the issues on TV, but Kennedy refused.

Kennedy won the Indiana Democratic Presidential primary May 7 in a contest against McCarthy and a favorite-son candidate, Gov. Roger D. Branigin. Kennedy received 320,485 votes (42%), Branigin 234,312 (31%) and McCarthy 209,165 (27%). By carrying 9 of the 11 Congressional districts (Branigin won the other 2), Kennedy was assured of most of the state's 63 convention votes on the first ballot, although the state Democratic committee was to determine later the manner in which the delegation vote would be distributed on a state-wide and district basis.

Kennedy won the Nebraska Democratic Presidential primary May 14. He received 52% of the vote. McCarthy was 2d with 31% of the vote. Vice Pres. Humphrey was 3d with 8% of the vote (write-ins). Pres. Johnson, who withdrew from the race too late for his name to be removed from the ballot, won 6% of the vote. Republican Richard Nixon received .8% of the Democratic vote on a write-in effort.

Peace Talks & Other Issues

Kennedy had blamed the Johnson Administration Apr. 18 for the delay in getting peace talks started. Speaking at Oregon State University in Corvallis, Kennedy said:

"2 weeks ago we were all enormously heartened by the President's initiative toward preliminary talks for peace. Yet despite our pledge again and again in the past several years to go 'anywhere, anytime' to seek a negotiated end to the war, these preliminary talks—much less genuine negotiations—have yet to begin. I think we should begin. I don't think that we should be responsible for continuing to raise other terms and other conditions in connection with the negotiations.

"We made our position clear a year ago. We made our position clear 2 years ago that we'd go anytime, any place. We didn't say we'd go any place but Pnompenh, or go any place but Warsaw. We didn't say at that time we'd only go if the South Koreans were present or the South Vietnamese were present. We said we wanted to talk about peace. I think we should go and talk about peace.

"Last week our combat deaths were the highest in 5 weeks. Once again, combat deaths were greater among Americans than in the ranks of the South Vietnamese army. And the other costs of the war also continue—to the South Vietnamese people and to our own country. The war still distracts us from our pressing domestic needs and our responsibilities elsewhere in the world. It still costs us $2.5 billion a month—$600 million a week. Every day the war is prolonged—whether by inability to reach agreement on a site for talks, or any other reason—every such delay costs us $85 million a day—more for every single day than the cost of a moderate program to bring jobs to young people in the ghetto for an entire summer all over America—a program we are now told we cannot afford.

"So we have to go working to assure that this war is honorably settled at the conference table—not in some indefinite future but while something still remains of the country of Vietnam and our own hopes for domestic progress."

In what his aides described as his most definitive campaign statement to date on foreign policy, Kennedy told students at Indiana University in Bloomington Apr. 24 that the U.S. should view its power to intervene in other nations' affairs "only as a strategic reserve against the most serious of threats." Unless America's "central interests" were directly threatened, "we should give no more assistance to a government against any internal threat than that government is capable of using itself," he said.

In his Indiana University talk, Kennedy rejected the "domino theory." Challenging a recent statement by State Undersecy. Nicholas DeB. Katzenbach that if Vietnam fell to the Communists, the rest of Southeast Asia might fall also, Kennedy said:

"Vietnam is only Vietnam. It will not settle the fate of Asia or America—much less the fate of the whole world."

At Purdue University May 1 Kennedy said that the U.S. should not be concerned about losing face by accepting North Vietnam's proposals on a site for peace talks: "After all, we are the strongest nation in the world. We are talking about where to meet to talk about whether serious negotiations are to take place—all with a nation less than 1/10 our size, with the merest fraction of our wealth, prestige and power." "We need not worry about whether we will lose face by agreeing to a site we have not suggested. The important thing—our responsibility to our own men and our own people—is to get the talks started and try to reach an honorable settlement to this costly and divisive war."

In most of his Indiana appearances Kennedy emphasized domestic policy, stressing the need for social justice and law and order. In his Purdue speech, however, he concentrated on getting peace talks started. "I do not underestimate the difficulties of agreement on a site that is both acceptable and accessible to all concerned," he said. "But neither do I underestimate the urgency of agreeing on a site and getting those preliminary talks under way. Each week of delay costs the lives of hundreds of men and further postpones our own hopes for domestic progress."

Kennedy had told students at San Francisco University Apr. 19 that he was against an amnesty for draft evaders or resisters. Throughout his speech and a question-and-answer period Kennedy was heckled by a small minority of the students who shouted pro-Viet Cong slogans and interrupted him continuously.

Kennedy criticized student draft deferments May 13 during a question-and-answer session with students at Creighton University in Omaha, Neb. A scattering of boos from the audience followed, and a student asked Kennedy whether the Army wasn't one way of getting young people out of the ghettos and solving the ghetto problem. Kennedy replied: "Here, at a Catholic university, how can you say that we can deal with the problems of the poor by sending them to Vietnam? There is a great moral force in the United States about the wrongs of the federal government and all the mistakes Lyndon Johnson has made and how Congress has failed to pass legislation dealing with civil rights; and yet when it comes down to you, your-selves and your own individual lives, then you say students should be draft-deferred."

Kennedy asked for a show of hands from those who favored student deferments. When about half the audience responded af-firmatively, Kennedy said: "Look around you. How many black faces do you see here, how many American Indians, how many Mexican-Americans?" "The fact is, if you look at any regiment or division of paratroopers in Vietnam, 45% of them are black. How can you accept this?" "What I don't understand is that you don't debate these things among yourselves." "You're the most exclusive minority in the world. Are you just going to sit on your duffs and do nothing or just carry signs and protest?"

Kennedy sought May 8 to differentiate between the Israeli cause and that of South Vietnam. Speaking in New York before the Synagogue Council of America, Kennedy said: "Israel is not Vietnam. Indeed it is the very opposite of Vietnam. Israel's government is democratic, effective, free of corruption; its people are united in its support. We can and we should help Israel; but we can do this, I believe, secure in the knowledge that the Israelis—as they made so courageously clear during the June war—will not ask us to do their job for them; whether the terms of decision are idealistic or practical, helping Israel is in our most basic interest."

McCarthy Upsets Kennedy in Oregon

McCarthy scored an upset victory over Kennedy May 28 in the Oregon primary. McCarthy received 45% of the vote, Kennedy 39%. Pres. Johnson, on the ballot before his withdrawal from the campaign, received 12% of the vote. Vice Pres. Humphrey received 4% through write-in votes. Richard Nixon won the Republican Presidential primary with 73% of the vote.

Kennedy's loss was the first election defeat of a member of the Kennedy family in 30 consecutive primary and general contests since 1946.

Both Kennedy and McCarthy had campaigned hard in Oregon. A week before the vote, McCarthy assailed Kennedy's record on Vietnam and repeatedly cited his offer, rejected by Kennedy, for a debate and confrontation. He also stressed that he was the first to challenge Pres. Johnson. These points were considered potent arguments in Oregon, where McCarthy had an efficient organization and sufficient funds, essentials reportedly lacking in some of his earlier primaries. McCarthy had criticized Humphrey and Kennedy during a KGW-TV interview in Portland May 22, attacking them for misguided views on the Vietnamese war. Humphrey, he said, presented the Administration's case "sometimes even more forcefully" than Johnson himself. Kennedy, he said, had come "very slowly to a position of opposition." Kennedy's record on Vietnam, McCarthy declared, "has been, until very recently, one of approving the involvement."

Kennedy had said at a San Francisco Press Club meeting May 21 that if he lost either the Oregon primary or the California one, "I'm not a very viable candidate." "I think I have to win in Oregon," he said in reply to a question following his speech. Speaking at Eastern Oregon College in La Grande May 22, Kennedy identified Humphrey as his "major opponent" in Oregon. In reply to a question about a Kennedy-McCarthy debate (McCarthy had challenged him), Kennedy said he had "opened myself to questions all across the state," and "it's not a question of my not giving my point of view." "If we are going to have a discussion," he said, "I think the Vice President should be there, because that's the key and the core and the heart of where the campaign is going, and what direction the Democratic Party is going, and what direction the country is going."

After experimenting with other issues for 2 weeks, Kennedy had concentrated on the war during the last 10 days of his Oregon campaign. He emphasized the limitations of the South Vietnamese government and the failure of its army to do more to win the war. Kennedy also assailed the over-all conduct of Johnson Administration foreign policy as reflecting "an obsession with power" and "with military matters." In what one reporter described as a "blatant pitch for the women's vote," Kennedy called for the appointment of a woman to the American negotiating team in Paris on the ground that "they're the ones who have to give their husbands. They're the ones who have to send their sons. They're the ones who are making such a great sacrifice in addition to the men in Vietnam."

Kennedy May 29 described his defeat in Oregon as a "setback I could ill afford" and indicated that his candidacy would stand or fall on the results of the California primary. "I will abide by the results of that test," he told newsmen in Los Angeles. In the aftermath of the Oregon vote, Kennedy reversed himself and agreed to debate McCarthy on TV. Kennedy deplored the prospect of a choice in the general election between Humphrey for the Democrats and Nixon for the Republicans. If Humphrey and Nixon were the choices, he said, the major parties would have failed "to offer the people a chance to move in a new and more hopeful direction" in foreign and domestic policy. He said there then would be no candidate "who has opposed the course of escalation of the war in Vietnam," who was "committed to the kinds of programs which can remedy the conditions which are transforming our cities into armed camps" or who was "committed to return government to the people" or to "returning to the economic policies which gave us rising prosperity without destructive inflation."

Kennedy told the newsmen, however, that he would support in the general election whoever was nominated for President at the Democratic Convention. That was the first time since he entered the race Mar. 16 that Kennedy stated unequivocally that he would support whomever the Democrats nominated for President. At the same news conference, Kennedy said that "under no circumstances" would he accept nomination for Vice President.

Kennedy Vs. McCarthy in California

Kennedy claimed May 31 that his opposition to the war predated McCarthy's. "I think we learned from that mistake [of massive intervention in South Vietnam], and that is why I spoke out in 1965, which I might say was earlier than any of the other men who are presently running" for President, he said in a departure from his prepared remarks in a speech at the Commonwealth Club in San Francisco. It was not clear what Sen. Kennedy had in mind in asserting that he had spoken out against the war in 1965. Appearing on the NBC-TV program "Meet the Press" Dec. 5, 1965, Kennedy had said that he "basically" supported Administration policy in Vietnam.

A TV "debate" between Kennedy and McCarthy highlighted the California primary campaign. The confrontation took place June 1 over the ABC network. An informal roundtable format was employed. Each candidate answered questions posed by 3 ABC reporters and was given a chance to comment on the other's answers. There were points of difference in their answers, but they seemed more in agreement than in disagreement on most issues. Observers concluded that neither had won a clear-cut victory in the debate.

One apparent difference in the positions of the 2 candidates concerned Vietnam. McCarthy said that a new "coalition" or "fusion" government in South Vietnam was a prerequisite for meaningful negotiations. Kennedy said that he was opposed to "forcing a coalition government on the government of Saigon ... before we begin the negotiations." McCarthy then denied that he wanted "to force a coalition on South Vietnam. I said we should make clear that we are willing to accept that," he said. "Now, if the South Vietnamese want to continue to fight, work out their own negotiation, that is well and good, but I don't think there is much point in talking about reform in Saigon or land reform because we have been asking for that for at least 5 years and it hasn't happened."

Each candidate was asked what he would do that Pres. Johnson was not doing to bring peace to Vietnam. Their answers were:

McCarthy—"There are 2 or 3 things that I would be doing, or at least recommending, if I were President..... I would be de-escalating the war in Vietnam, drawing back from some of our advanced positions, while still holding strength in Vietnam. I would not have the Secretary of State making statements about how we would have no coalition government to come out of the conference in Paris, nor have someone saying that the Vice President made a slip of the tongue when he talked about involving the National Liberation Front.

"I think these are the important positions that have to be taken: one, a de-escalation of the war; and secondly, a recognition that we have to have a new government in South Vietnam. I am not particularly concerned whether it is called a coalition or a fusion or a new government of some kind. And we have to recognize that that government would include the National Liberation Front. I think this is prerequisite to any kind of negotiations that may move on to talk about what the nature of that new government might be. We have not really made any significant changes that I can see in terms of our activities or our words. We are calling up more troops. We say we are going to send more troops. We have intensified the bombing. So that taken all together, I don't see, either in action or in word, any significant change on the part of the Administration since the negotiations began."

Kennedy—"Well, I would pursue the negotiations in Paris. At the same time I would make it quite clear that we would expect that Saigon, the government in Saigon, would begin their own negotiations with the National Liberation Front.

"I would be opposed to what I understand Sen. McCarthy's position is, of forcing a coalition government on the government of Saigon, a coalition with the Communists, even before we begin the negotiations.

"I would make it quite clear that we are going to the negotiating table, not with the idea that we want them to unconditionally surrender, and that we expect that the National Liberation Front and the Viet Cong will play some role in the future political process of South Vietnam, but that should be determined by the negotiators and particularly by those people of South Vietnam. I think that is terribly important that we accept that because, without accepting that, what we are really asking for is unconditional surrender and they are not going to turn over their arms, lay down their arms, live in peace, if the votes and the government are going to be run by Gen. Ky and Gen. Thieu.

"The next point I would demand privately and publicly, an end of public corruption, the official corruption that exists in Vietnam, a land-reform program that is meaningful so that they can gain the support of the people themselves.

"I would pull back from the demilitarized zone. I think that is an important area, but I would permit the troops of South Vietnam to remain there rather than American troops, where 1/3 of our casualties have really occurred, and I would end the search and destroy missions by American troops and American Marines and let the South Vietnamese soldiers and troops carry that burden of the conflict.

"I would make it clear as we went along that the South Vietnamese are going to carry more and more of the burden of conflict. I am not going to accept the idea that we can draft the young men from the United States, send them to South Vietnam to fight and maybe to die, while at the same time a young man, if he is wealthy enough, can buy his way out of the draft in South Vietnam.

Appearing on the CBS-TV program "Face the Nation" June 2, McCarthy said that to leave to the South Vietnamese government the decision on a coalition government, as Kennedy suggested, would simply "put us right back where we are." Later that day, in a panel discussion on KRON-TV in San Francisco, McCarthy said that "He [Kennedy] said that he wouldn't force a coalition. I feel that, directly or indirectly, that's what we have to do."

Kennedy Wins—& Dies—in California

Kennedy defeated McCarthy—46% to 42%—in the California primary June 4, thereby winning 172 Democratic National Convention delegate votes. A 3d slate of delegates, headed by state Atty. Gen. Thomas C. Lynch, received 12% of the total Democratic vote. The Lynch slate included supporters of both Senators and of Vice Pres. Humphrey. Kennedy's victory was attributed to a heavy vote from minority groups—Negroes and Mexican-Americans—and from labor. He received large pluralities in the Los Angeles, San Francisco and Sacramento areas to overcome the statewide strength shown by McCarthy, who won more counties than did Kennedy.

Kennedy's 80-day campaign for the Presidency ended just after that midnight at 12:16 PDT June 5, 1968 when he was shot by Sirhan B. Sirhan in a Los Angeles hotel minutes after he had claimed victory in the California primary. The Senator died 26 hours later without regaining consciousness. 2 days later Robert Kennedy's coffin was lowered into a grave in the same Arlington, Va. hillside where his brother John had been buried in Nov. 1963.

EDWARD
MOORE
KENNEDY

Edward M. Kennedy

HEIR TO THE KENNEDY TRADITION

Following the assassination of a 2d Kennedy, widespread attention focused on the sole surviving brother as the heir and upholder of what had come to be considered a family tradition. Edward Moore Kennedy—whose nickname Ted seemed almost custom-made for headlines—already occupied the Senate seat that had once been filled by the late John Kennedy. It was generally acknowledged that he would succeed Robert Kennedy as a strong prospective contender for a Democratic Presidential nomination. And he was quickly accepted as a leader of the forces demanding fast action for peace in Vietnam.

Edward Kennedy's Peace Plan

In his first public appearance since Robert Kennedy's assassination, Edward Kennedy Aug. 21, 1968 proposed a 4-point plan to end the Vietnamese war, which he termed "the tragedy of our generation." Kennedy presented his proposals in a speech before the Chamber of Commerce in Worcester, Mass.

To bring an end to the conflict, Kennedy declared, the U.S., "as soon as possible," should: (1) "end unconditionally all bombing of North Vietnam"; (2) "negotiate with Hanoi the mutual withdrawal from South Vietnam of all foreign forces, both allied and North Vietnamese"; (3) "accompany this withdrawal with whatever help we can give to the South Vietnamese in the building of a viable political economic and legal structure that will not promptly collapse upon our departure"; (4) "demonstrate to both Hanoi and Saigon the sincerity of our intentions by significantly decreasing this year the level of our military activity and military personnel in the South." Under his plan, he said, the U.S. could end its involvement in the war "with honor," and the Paris peace talks would not founder on the problems of a coalition government, election procedures or the make-up of future cabinets in South Vietnam.

Kennedy defended the call for a bombing halt by saying that the bombing had not reduced the movement of enemy troops and materiel and that "an end to the killing in Vietnam can never be negotiated as long as the bombing of North Vietnam continues." "Halting the bombing would thus save many more American lives than it would ever endanger," he declared.

According to Kennedy, the U.S. could help build a Vietnamese society, but it must make clear to the South Vietnamese government "our intention to withdraw from the South as Hanoi withdraws" and "our complete unwillingness thereafter to bear the burden of their responsibility and pick up the pieces of their failure." Saigon "must not be given a veto over our course in Paris, our cessation of the bombing, or our mutual withdrawal of troops," he said. "They must be given clear notice that their chief prop will be taken away as soon as we can conclude such negotiations with Hanoi."

Kennedy asserted that the hopes of the U.S. in its effort to help South Vietnam "build a nation" had "foundered in miscalculation and self-deception," had been "stymied by the stubbornness of the foe, but, above all, ... [had] been buried by the incompetence and corruption of our South Vietnamese allies."

Earlier in 1968, in his first book, *Decisions for a Decade,* Edward Kennedy had proposed that if negotiations were not forthcoming, the U.S. should adopt a "military posture designed to protect and hold secure areas of heavy population in order to maximize the safety and security of the Vietnamese people rather than to search out and destroy the enemy." Kennedy also urged that the U.S. "settle" with the South Vietnamese "the entire question of their corruption, inefficiency and the waste of American resources and the future of the pacification program." According to Kennedy: "We should do all that is necessary to help the Saigon government prepare to take over its responsibilities, but if they are unwilling to do so, they should know that the American people, with great justification, could well consider our responsibilities fulfilled."

Kennedy-Backed Plank Defeated at Convention

The Democratic National Convention met in Chicago Aug. 26-29, 1968, nominated Hubert H. Humphrey for President and adopted a party platform plank indorsing the Johnson Administration's Vietnam policies. An anti-Administration plank sponsored by Sens. Eugene McCarthy, George McGovern and Edward Kennedy was defeated by a vote of 1,567-3/4 to 1,041-1/4 after a 3-hour debate punctuated by chants of "Stop the war!"

The McCarthy-McGovern-Kennedy plank, presented as a minority report of the platform committee, called for: (a) an unconditional cessation of all bombing of North Vietnam; (b) negotiation of a phased, mutual withdrawal of U.S. and North Vietnamese troops from South Vietnam; (c) encouragement of South Vietnam "to negotiate a political reconciliation with the National Liberation Front looking toward a ... broadly representative" government for South Vietnam, and (d) reduction of U.S. offensive operations in South Vietnam, "thus enabling an early withdrawal of a significant number of our troops."

The Johnson-Humphrey plank, presented as the majority choice of the platform committee, advocated: (a) a halt in the bombing of North Vietnam "when this action would not endanger the lives of our troops in the field" and would "take into account the response from Hanoi"; (b) withdrawal of all foreign forces from South Vietnam only after negotiating "with Hanoi an immediate end or limitation of hostilities," and (c) establishment of a postwar government by free elections with international supervision and participation open to all who "accept peaceful political processes." The plank "applaud[ed] the initiative of Pres. Johnson which brought North Vietnam to the peace table" and called on Hanoi to "respond positively to this act of statesmanship."

Kennedy Criticizes Nixon's Vietnam Policies

The new Nixon Administration's Vietnam policies came under frequent attack by Edward Kennedy beginning in the Spring of 1969.

In a Senate speech May 20, 1969, Kennedy denounced the U.S. fight for Apbia Mountain (Hamburger Hill) in South Vietnam as "senseless and irresponsible." U.S. and South Vietnamese forces captured the mountain May 20 by fighting one of the bloodiest battles of the war; 50 U.S. soldiers were killed and 270 wounded. In the aftermath of the 10-day battle Kennedy called for "a new order to the field cutting back these offensive operations." "Pres. Nixon has told us, without question, that we seek no military victory, that we seek only peace," Kennedy said. "How then can we justify sending our boys against a hill a dozen times or more, until soldiers themselves question the madness of the action? The assault on Hamburger Hill is only symptomatic of a mentality and a policy that requires immediate attention. The American lives are too valuable to be sacrificed for military pride." The level of U.S. field operations "runs opposite to our stated intentions and goals in Paris," Kennedy declared.

An immediate rebuttal to Kennedy's speech was given by Senate Republican whip Hugh Scott (R., Pa.), who told the Senate he would not try to "2d-guess" battlefield tactics. "If our military are told to contend for a hill, it is part of the strategy which is essential to maintaining the military posture while we talk for peace." Kennedy's remarks were denounced again in the Senate May 26 by Sens. Margaret Chase Smith (R., Me.), John G. Tower (R., Tex.) and Harry Byrd Jr. (D., Va.).

Kennedy returned to the theme in addressing the New Democratic Coalition in Washington May 24. Deploring the "cruelty and savagery of the past week," he said "it would have been immoral if we remained silent" about "an unjustified war, an immoral war." "We do have a responsibility in demilitarizing that war and bringing our boys home," he said. The war "contaminates our atmosphere.... It separates our young." Another speaker at the meeting, Sen. George S. McGovern (D., S.D.), commended Kennedy "for raising his voice ... eloquently ... in protest against a truly senseless slaughter."

Kennedy Sept. 18, 1969 strongly condemned the Nixon Administration's over-all war policies. He simultaneously assailed the South Vietnamese government of Pres. Nguyen Van Thieu, which he called "corrupt and repressive." These attacks were made in a Boston speech—Kennedy's first political appearance since a July car accident that resulted in the death of his passenger, Mary Jo Kopechne. Kennedy said that despite the 1968 Presidential election and "the promises of a new President and ... new rhetoric, the war in Vietnam is virtually unchanged." Kennedy asserted that the Nixon policy "is the road to war, and war and more war. And as we follow this incredible path it will continue to erode the health, the economy and the moral and spiritual strength of the United States of America." The Administration's troop withdrawals were "token," "more an exercise in politics and improvisation while the level of fighting and casualties continues," he charged. The refusal to compromise on the issue of a coalition government for South Vietnam, Kennedy said, was asking the enemy "to accept defeat and we have not defeated them."

"We have not been willing to consider the continued control of the Thieu regime as a negotiable question." Kennedy continued, "and ... as long as we remain unmoved on this issue there can be no peaceful solution. ... It is time to say to the Saigon government, 'If you will not agree to a sensible compromise—even if it endangers your personal power—then it is your war and you must fight it alone.'"

One of the most massive series of antiwar protests in U.S. history took place Oct. 15 as part of an effort to convince Nixon of a wide public demand that he end the war. The event—planned and coordinated by a Vietnam Moratorium Committee in Washington, D.C.— drew diverse support from thousands of students and other youths, professors and clergymen as well as many representatives of the middle class who generally had remained aloof from public opposition to the war effort. One of the largest of the gatherings was the one in Boston, where an estimated 100,000 persons gathered on Boston Common. At the rally Kennedy proposed a "hard compromise" under which the U.S. would withdraw its ground combat forces from Vietnam within a year and its air and support units by the end of 1972.

Nixon Sets Timetable for U.S. Pullout

In a nationally televised speech on Vietnam Nov. 3, 1969, Nixon said his Administration had adopted a plan, in cooperation with the South Vietnamese, for the complete withdrawal of all U.S. ground combat forces "on an orderly scheduled timetable." But he refused to divulge the timetable on the ground that it would remove the enemy's incentive to negotiate. They "would simply wait until our forces had withdrawn and then move in," he said.

Nixon appealed for national unity in support of his Vietnam policies and asserted that "North Vietnam cannot defeat or humiliate the United States; only Americans can do that." He directed a special plea to "the great silent majority of my fellow Americans" for support. "I pledged in my campaign for the Presidency to end the war in a way that we could win the peace," he said. "I have initiated a plan of action which will enable me to keep that pledge. The more support I can have from the American people, the sooner that pledge can be redeemed. For the more divided we are at home, the less likely the enemy is to negotiate in Paris."

Edward Kennedy denounced Pres. Nixon's speech Nov. 4. Speaking in the Senate, Kennedy said that "there now must be doubt whether there is in existence any plan to extricate America from this war." Kennedy said in his Nov. 4 speech:

"... I and millions of Americans were most disappointed by the President's address.... The President's speech, simply stated, was more of the same—no new hopes, no new considerations, no new inspiration for an American people who have waited so long and given so much for peace.

"... The time has come to say it: As a candidate, Richard Nixon promised us a plan for peace once elected; as chief executive, Pres. Nixon promised us a plan for peace for the last 10 months. Last night he spoke again of a plan—a secret plan for peace sometime. There now must be doubt whether there is in existence any plan to extricate America from this war in the best interest of America—for it is no plan to say that what we will do depends upon what Hanoi does. In effect, the President has passed all decision-making power for peace over to the government of Hanoi—if they wish the fighting to subside it will subside, if they wish the war to escalate, it will escalate. At this late hour of war and killing and violence, I find that position to be both tragic and unacceptable.

"I feel that the people of this country had a right to expect more of their leader than a simple reiteration of the past. To say there must be more war to prove our fidelity to friends after 6 years of war is but rhetoric; to hold out the possibility of the horror of killing in Vietnam after we leave, as a reason why we must continue the killing, is almost beyond comment. And so this Administration, by clinging to the policies of the past when the time for peace has come, must expect that those who feel differently will rise to this test. The call for unity cannot be responsibly heeded when a leadership has exhibited no policy or plan that unifies. It is difficult to ask a people to join in support of a position that is no different from that which has split our country before.

"I do not feel that the war in Vietnam is worth thousands more American lives. Yet we have been given no indication that there now exists any limit to the number of lives or amount of resources that this country will expend to preserve the government of Saigon. If real negotiations and peace were more important to us than the continued personal power of Pres. Thieu and the Saigon regime, the Aug. 25 letter from Hanoi could have been seized as an opening, not a closing, of communication between adversaries. If that chance is now gone, and the only alternative is war and more war, then there is little hope that the burden of Vietnam will be lifted from America in the near future."

Kennedy Urges U.S. to Quit Southeast Asia

Kennedy asserted Apr. 3, 1970 that the time had come for the U.S. to begin "to militarily get out of Southeast Asia lock, stock and barrel." Speaking in Peabody, Mass. at a dinner for Rep. Michael Harrington (D., Mass.), Kennedy said that the pace of U.S. troop withdrawals from Vietnam indicated that the "war is far from over." He called the President's Vietnamization policy a plan of "continued war with a lessening of tensions here in the U.S." That policy "is based on the hope of military success in a struggle that knows no such solution," Kennedy declared. Kennedy also said:

"Yesterday Massachusetts produced a most basic, a most serious challenge to an Executive act that has cost thousands and thousands of lives and billions of dollars—by attacking its very legality.* But the Commonwealth has a history of speaking its mind on matters of war and peace. During the War of 1812, the Massachusetts Lower House passed a manifesto urging the organization of a peace party and stating, 'Let there be no volunteers' for the war. Shortly thereafter Gov. Caleb Strong refused to call the state militia into national service; while our legislature rejected a vote of thanks to a military hero as 'not becoming a moral and religious people.'

"That was long ago, and the causes were very different from those creating our most recent action. But the feeling may well have been the same—this business of war, of killing, of maiming, is so contrary to humanity that it must always be open to question and challenge in a free society. So again today Massachusetts is formally challenging a war. How deep our feelings must be about Vietnam, how wounded must be the American spirit that a legislature would feel forced to act in this fashion. The full cost of Vietnam may truly never be known or accounted for in our lifetime; but we have already begun paying the price in the cynicism of our youth, the division of our races, and in the decaying mounds we call our cities.

"When will it end? When will we free ourselves from this great error that has brought us so low, sapping our vitality and placing even our simplest hopes for America in doubt?

"At the current rate of withdrawal, and if we were to remove all American troops, we would still be involved in a Vietnam war for 3 more years. And if it is true that we may stop our withdrawals at a level of 200,000 men, the future of our involvement is openended. If the war continues, as it must under our present policy, the next 3 years could cost us approximately $60 billion, anywhere from 10,000 to 12,000 more American lives, and hundreds of thousands of Vietnamese deaths.... But what if the pace of withdrawal is slowed? What if we commit more resources to Laos? What if the Cambodian situation causes us to treat all problems in the larger context of Indochina? Given the history of our activities in Southeast Asia, can we afford to treat these additional possibilities as unrealistic? I, for one, do not believe we can. They are most realistic possibilities; and the

---

*The Massachusetts law, an attempt to test the constitutionality of the war, held that Massachusetts citizens could not be ordered to Vietnam without Congressional action. When the state took its case to the U.S. Supreme Court, however, the court Nov. 9, 1970 ruled 6 to 3 that it would not hear the matter.

slightest weakening of our resolve to remove ourselves from Vietnam makes meaningless all future estimates of death, destruction and cost.

"The simple truth is that this war is far from over. It is time for the American public to shake off the lethargy of the past 15 months.

"Vietnamization has nothing to do with peace. It is a policy of continued war with a lessening of tensions here in the United States. It is based on the hope of military success in a struggle that knows no such solution. It condemns a country—Vietnam—to more violence, more death, more refugees. It holds out false hopes to both the American public and the people of Vietnam. And it is a policy that at any moment can come tumbling down about our ears, giving renewed reason for further, or more prolonged, U.S. involvement.

"... Vietnamization is a misguided and inhuman policy, constructed only to avoid the hard political realities that could have been faced by a new President....

"It is not too late. The Administration can still face the question that when properly answered could end the violence. *Are we as a nation prepared to see a future government in Saigon that contains elements in it unfriendly to us?* If the answer is yes, then let us get on with the negotiations, for that is what this terrible war is all about. We have not defeated the enemy, we cannot defeat the enemy without annihilating a whole people. Military victory is not even our stated goal. For how much longer, then, will we allow our youth to die to avoid the hard, but ultimate, political conclusion?

"Apparently, other things remaining equal, they will be allowed to die for a few more years. But other things will not remain equal. Vietnam will burst upon the American consciousness again, and this government, like the one before it, will reap the bitter harvest of dissent and division. But more importantly, our nation will be further crippled, our problems further magnified, distrust of our institutions will grow deeper and deeper, and repression will be the antidote freely employed.

"This month may produce the signs of what is to come. Further troop withdrawals are scheduled to be announced. The President is receiving anew pleas from the military for more time. The loss of the Plain of Jars in Laos and increased North Vietnamese pressure there will cause a new argument for delay, as will the current instability in Cambodia. To falter at this moment, even in the pursuit of what is called Vietnamization, could be a disastrous act of hesitancy. The pace of withdrawal, even at only 12,000 men a month, must be maintained as a minimum act of keeping faith with the American people.

"But it is, indeed, a minimal act. We can no longer keep coasting on this matter of death in Vietnam, hoping the domestic lull here at home will remain. Changes must be made, not only in elevating the level of our Paris negotiators but in refreshing our embassy in Saigon. Changes must be made in our relations with the government of South Vietnam—a government whose best interests are not consistent with our best interests, a government not at all committed to the values for which our men are dying. We must make it clear to all concerned that we are now ready for true political negotiations to end a political war. We must make it clear that our goal is an end to violence through real compromise. Absent this, we are doomed to continue throwing our resources—men and machines—into a pit. We are doomed, not just to wage an undeclared war, but even a secret one in Laos. We spend $2 billion a year bombing the Ho Chi Minh Trail and the countryside of Northern Laos—8,000 sorties a month on the trail, 4,000 sorties elsewhere in support of Laotian troops, not to mention the loss of pilots as yet undetermined. And it is quite possible, despite all statements to the contrary, that if pressure mounts on the handful of troops known as Cambodia's army, we will find ourselves stretched to their support or defense.

"So this is the time for decisions that could affect us for a decade or more. This is the time to begin, as the majority leader [Sen. Mike Mansfield] of the Senate said, to militarily get out of Southeast Asia, lock, stock and barrel. Events are occurring there that are not in our control and, as history will show, never were in our control. But even if that is in question, I am quite satisfied that events are occurring there that are not related to the national security interests of the United States. We must, in short, cease taking and losing human life in that small place on this earth.

"Perhaps the action of the Massachusetts State Legislature this week marks the end to a difficult time. Since the fall of Eastern Europe after the 2d World War we lived with a cold war mentality and the concurrent growth of Presidential power to support its policies. Now we suffer its final throes in the deltas and highlands of old Indochina. I fervently hope it is the end of an era that caused us to place our reliance on the military in an overly simplistic view of our world. For we have a nation right here to put back together again, a people to join, a society that must be mended. It is time to begin all that."

Kennedy's contention that the U.S. should "begin militarily to get out of Southeast Asia lock, stock and barrel" was manifest in his support in the Senate of the Cooper-Church and McGovern-Hatfield amendments. The Cooper-Church amendment was attached to a foreign military sales bill authorizing $300 million in credit sales of arms to foreign countries. The amendment sought "to expedite the withdrawal of American forces from Cambodia" following Nixon's sending of American troops into Cambodia May 1 for the announced purpose of destroying Communist supplies.

The amendment provided that no funds could be expended after July 1, 1970 for the purposes of: (1) Retaining United States forces in Cambodia; (2) paying the compensation or allowances of, or otherwise supporting, directly or indirectly, any U.S. personnel in Cambodia who furnished military instruction to Cambodian forces or engaged in any combat activity in support of Cambodian forces; (3) entering into or carrying out any contract or agreement to provide military instruction in Cambodia, or to provide persons to engage in any combat activity in support of Cambodian forces; or (4) conducting any combat activity in the air above Cambodia in direct support of Cambodian forces. A provision stated that the amendment did not seek "to impugn the constitutional power of the President as commander-in-chief, including the exercise of that constitutional power which may be necessary to protect the lives of United States armed forces wherever deployed."

The Cooper-Church amendment was passed by 58-37 Senate vote June 30, 1970. Sen. Kennedy was one of 42 Democrats and 16 Republicans to vote for the amendment. On the day the amendment was passed by the Senate, the Pentagon announced that U.S. forces had completed their withdrawal from Cambodia.

The Hatfield - McGovern "amendment to end the war" in Vietnam was rejected by 55-39 Senate vote Sept. 1, 1970. Kennedy was one of 32 Democrats and 7 Republicans who voted for the amendment.

The amendment, proposed by Sens. Mark O. Hatfield and George S. McGovern, provided that no more than 280,000 U.S. troops could be retained in South Vietnam after Apr. 30, 1971 and that all U.S. troops would have to be withdrawn by the end of 1971. In the event of an "unanticipated clear and present danger," the amendment provided that the President could keep the troops in Vietnam for 60 more days and submit to Congress a request for authorization of a new total withdrawal date.

Rejection of the amendment was seen as an Administration victory and Senate support for Nixon's Indochina policy. But some doves voted against the amendment, including Sen. John Sherman Cooper (R., Ky.), who believed there would be a better chance for negotiations if the proposal were not adopted. In arguing against adoption, Sen. John C. Stennis (D., Miss.) told the Senate prior to the vote that the move was constitutional and Congress had "the sole power to appropriate money." But, he urged, "Let's not stampede, let's go on down the road with whatever power our chief executive has as a negotiator, as a man of discernment."

McGovern, in his final argument, said: "Every Senator in this chamber is partly responsible for sending 50,000 young Americans to an early grave and ... for that human wreckage at Walter Reed [hospital] and all across this land—young boys without legs, without arms, or genitals, or faces, or hopes. If we don't end this damnable war those young men will some day curse us for our pitiful willingness to let the Executive [branch] carry the burden that the Constitution places on us."

The vote on the Hatfield-McGovern amendment climaxed the protracted debate on a $19.2 billion military procurement bill, which was approved later Sept. 1 by 84-5 vote and sent to conference with the House.

The Hatfield-McGovern amendment was one of several proposed amendments to the military procurement bill that sought to modify U.S. policies in Vietnam. An amendment to halt the use of herbicides in Vietnam to destroy foliage and enemy rice was rejected 62-22 Aug. 26. Kennedy voted against the measure, which had been introduced by Sens. Charles Goodell and Gaylord Nelson. An amendment to bar the use of herbicides on food crops in Vietnam was rejected 48-33 Aug. 27. Kennedy voted for the amendment. The Senate Sept. 1 voted 71-22 to bar sending draftees to Indochina against their will. Kennedy voted against that proposal on the ground that it "is directly contrary to one of the primary purposes of the draft—which is to assure that the burdens of war are, to the greatest extent possible, shared equally by all our citizens." He added: "I also have the feeling that this amendment would be self-defeating and would create enormous confusion. The draft would become the haven for war-dodgers, and the number of volunteers would rapidly decline. In all probability, it would soon become necessary to subject draftees to combat duties once again. We would be right back where we started with a great deal of dashed hopes and administrative inconvenience."

Attack on U.S. Operation in Cambodia

Kennedy bitterly and repeatedly denounced Pres. Nixon's sending of U.S. and South Vietnamese forces into Cambodia Apr. 30, 1970 for the announced purpose of seizing Communist supplies and command headquarters.

In an address to advertising and broadcasting executives in Boston May 1, Kennedy denounced the "increasing level of violence and expansion of war." In sending troops into Cambodia, Kennedy charged, Nixon "has fallen prey to the illusion that drove another from office—the illusion of an American military victory in Southeast Asia."

Speaking before the Massachusetts Dental Society in Boston May 5, Kennedy said: "The strange and tragic fascination of military victory in Vietnam has now cast its mad spell over 2 successive Presidents," while at home, "4 American students lie dead in Ohio on the playing fields of their university, slain in the heart of middle America by the violent temper of our society—slain as surely as if we ourselves had pulled the triggers of the rifles of the National Guard. Who of us, seeing American troops in Ohio fire wildly into a crowd of students, does not also see Mylai, with its defenseless Vietnamese civilians cut down by American troops? Can any of us fail to realize now what Vietnam has done to our spirit, our nation, and our sons?"

At Johns Hopkins University May 6, Kennedy said: The American people "seemed to conclude that Vietnam as a fact of life was on the wane. So certain were many that the matter had been settled that we celebrated Earth Day ... and turned our minds to inner tubes and beer cans, auto exhaust and smoke stacks." But Cambodia changed that. "In retrospect, what right had this nation to expect that those enamored with the illusion of military victory would acquiesce to our fondest dreams? Who ever guaranteed us that the chauvinistic phrases about the flag, about protecting our boys, about my country right or wrong, were carefully wrapped and stored away?"

Kennedy spoke in Washington, D.C. May 8 at a memorial service for 4 students killed by National Guardsmen during antiwar disturbances at Kent State University May 4. "Our prayer tonight is a simple one," he said. "Dear God, help us, this war must end."

THOMPSON, Sir Robert—55
THOUSAND Days, A (book)—47
THUAN, Nguyen Dinh—21
TIME (magazine)—77, 84, 111
TITO, Marshal (Josip Broz): 'Titoism'—8
TO Seek a Newer World (book)—105
TODAY (NBC-TV program)—78
TOWER, Sen. John G. (R., Tex.)—133
TRINH, Nguyen Duy—84, 103
TRUCES—68-9, 87, 95-6, 98, 104, 118. See also BOMBING Halts
TRUMAN, Harry S.—6-7
TUSCALOOSA, Ala.—114

U

UNION of Soviet Socialist Republics—5, 16, 18, 61, 64, 73, 75-6, 89, 91-2, 95-6, 99, 107
UNITED Nations (UN)—21, 60, 64, 71, 94
UNITED States: Note—Because this book is, largely, a record of U.S. military, political and policy developments, most items involving the U.S. are indexed under the subjects or names of the persons involved (e. g., BOMBING Halts). Aid & support (for South Vietnam)—13-5, 17, 19-29, 33, 35, 37-8, 41-2, 44, 46-50, 55-7, 66, 68, 75, 81, 92, 102, 104, 106, 113, 116-7, 122, 132, 137-8. Armistice—See CEASE-Fire(s). Cambodia — See CAMBODIA. Casualties—17, 32, 34, 37, 100, 116, 122, 127, 139. Congress—See CONGRESS. Counterinsurgency warfare—10, 24-5, 31-5, 55-6, 59, 63, 70. Helicopters—See HELICOPTERS. House of Representatives—See CONGRESS or specific member. Military Advisory Group (MAG)—22, 24. Military Assistance Command (MAC)—28. Military involvement (in Vietnam)—11-6, 17, 19, 21, 24-7, 29-37, 39, 41-2, 44-6, 55-62, 70-2, 78, 82, 89-97, 99, 102, 133, 135-6, 138-9; U.S. troop increases & withdrawals—17, 24, 30, 35, 37, 44-5, 48-9, 56-7, 83, 93, 117, 134, 136-9. Senate—See CONGRESS or specific member. State Department —See STATE, Department of, under 'S'

U.S. NEWS and World Report (magazine)—80
USSR—See UNION of Soviet Socialist Republics

V

VANDERBILT University—114-5
VENEZUELA—63, 66
VIET Cong—17-8, 25, 28-9, 33, 37-40, 46-7, 61, 63, 65-6, 68-9, 71, 78, 82-3, 90, 92, 94, 98, 104, 113, 126. Coalition government (proposed by Robert F. Kennedy)—73-81. Defection rates—33. Tet (1968) offensive—104, 114
VIET Minh—6, 8, 11-3, 18
VIETNAM—1, 5-6, 8-9, 11-2, 14, 65, 139. Division supported by Kennedy (John F.)—12. French war efforts collapse—11. See also ASIA, Southeast; INDOCHINA, Associated States of
VIETNAM, North—16, 23, 31, 42, 55, 60, 62, 68, 73, 75-6, 81-2, 84, 99, 101, 103-4, 117, 131-3, 135. Bombing (by U.S.)—60-1, 63, 67-71, 73, 81-4, 87, 89-90, 92-9, 101, 103-4, 106-7, 111, 117-8, 126, 131-2; bombing halts—69-70, 87, 89-97, 117-8. Peace efforts—98, 118
VIETNAM, South—13, 23, 63, 131-3. Casualties—18, 32-4, 65, 102. Ceasefires (truces)—68-9, 87, 95-6, 98, 104, 118. Coalition government proposal (Robert F. Kennedy)—73-81. Corruption & fraud—100-1, 105, 112-3, 123, 127, 132. Coups d'etat—29, 40-3, 46-8, 59, 113. Draft policy—101, 106-7, 110, 113, 115-6, 127. Elections—78, 100-1. Guerrilla warfare—See GUERRILLA Warfare. Looting — 107, 114. Presidential palace bombing—29. U.S. aid—See 'Aid,' etc. under UNITED States. U.S. combat training missions—17, 19, 21, 24-7, 30-7, 39, 41-2, 44-6, 48, 55-61, 102; see also UNITED States.
VIETNAM Moratorium Committee—134
VIETNAMIZATION Policy—136-9
VINH Long—34
VOICE of America—26, 44

W

WALINSKY, Adam—63
WALL Street Journal (newspaper)—30, 83